The Five Principles of Everything

ISBN 978-0-9853276-0-6

Published in the United States by Five Birds Industries, Laguna Woods, California

The opinions expressed in this book are solely those of the author and his various contributors.

Published in the United States of America.

Five Birds Publishing
603-G Avenida Sevilla
Laguna Woods, CA 92637

2011
First Edition

The Five Principles of Everything

by

Gordon Richiusa

Acknowledgements

I want to thank Dennis Mulkey, Jenny Garbus and Maria Arvelo for helping me to prepare the final draft of the *original* manuscript, and Alfred Urquidez and Edward Tao for their efforts to translate this one into Spanish and Chinese (respectively). Some of the original artwork, the picture of the raven and eagle flying together, as well as the hawk and the vulture portraits, for instance were produced by Darlene Marcos as wall paintings. All the original photos were taken and/or modeled by Gordon, Travis or Barbara Richiusa. In this book there are additional articles, lectures and abstracts that have been contributed by those admired and recognized as experts in their various fields. These contributors include (in alphabetical order): Maria Arvelo, Renee Baribeau, Russ Buchanan, Rick Burgin, Frank Dux, Steve Galvanoni, John Gates, Lisa Gates, John Harrison, Jhoon Rhee, Barbara Rich, Dana Stamos, Edward Tao, Alfred Urquidez, Ralph Villani, and Brian Wallace. This special note of thanks to these contributors is not enough to express my profound gratitude. It is these contributions that truly make this book valuable.

Front cover design: Jessie Horsting
Back cover photographer: Travis Richiusa

Table of Contents

An Introductory Overview

Human beings look for patterns in things. That is a fact that is accepted by scientists who study such things. We look for patterns as a way of trying to make sense of our lives. The desire to look for solutions to problems by finding a connection between things is, in a sense, in our DNA. This driving force in our humanity sometimes causes us to look for *and even believe we have found* patterns where there are none. However, usually if we find patterns and others find the same patterns (even if we were the first to notice these patterns) then we call that building consensus or acknowledged agreement and we determine that the pattern is valid or real. From these agreements we look for ways to make our individual lives better. Making things better is also something that seems to be ingrained in our DNA. Finally, while human beings are geared toward invention, when new data is added to any equation, our point of view or perspective is rightfully altered. When conditions change sufficiently to warrant an adjustment, human beings are also great re-inventors. In this first paragraph, I contextualize the five principles of everything and demonstrate the format for this book.

This book has grown from the original at the request of students of the basic concepts. In other words, the pattern was built upon the foundation of consensus. Originally, I presented The Five Principles of Everything as my personal blueprint for life (I'll return to that general image later) that I developed in the course of my studying the martial arts.

Over the years, I have worn many figurative hats. I've been a teacher, father, husband, friend, enemy, counselor, business owner, and freelance writer. Several of my first real jobs were in the field of writing and editing, in fact. I was a staff person, for instance at the original version of STAR Magazine, for Peterson Publishing on Sunset Blvd. in Hollywood. I also was the entire staff of editors and writers for Associated Valley Publications, where I performed the function of editor, layout artist, headline writer and journalist (using a number of pseudonyms).

To paraphrase Dustin Hoffman's character in the movie, ***Little Big Man***, "*then there was my lifeguard period.*" As a fairly decent swimmer, who had the good fortune to grow up in Southern California with a swimming pool in my parents' back-yard, I took the logical step of applying for a County Lifeguard position when I was in my teens. I passed the test, but was never hired for a position, because I landed a cushier lifeguard job at the Sportsman Lodge in North Hollywood.

There was rarely more than one person in the pool at a time, but I'm proud to say that in my many years of lifeguarding, I only had one incident where I needed to enter the water.

Because one lifeguard job led to another (and I was always looking for jobs where I could leave at quitting time and focus my attention on getting my degree or studying martial arts) I ended up taking a position at a home for emotionally disturbed children in Lake View Terrace, California. It was at this job that I began to logically apply the principles that would later become my *Five Principles of Chi.*

It seemed to me, at the time, that a good lifeguard was one who never had to put his own life in jeopardy to protect others. My main concern was the prevention of dangerous situations. For instance, I made certain that everyone who entered the pool I was guarding could swim. If they could not, then they were required to take swimming lessons (which I supplied). I even organized the staff to learn water safety and taught the Red Cross approved lifeguard classes for them. It never hurts to have help in whatever we are doing, and when the house-parents (what the live-in counselors were called) would bring twenty emotionally disturbed children with them to the pool, it made my job easier if they were also card-carrying lifeguards. Eventually, the season for swimming ended and I become a houseparent myself, and then an assistant-supervisor of a living unit where I was asked to “set an example” for the other staff. For some reason the work appealed to me and led me to work in lock-up facilities (Van Nuys Psychiatric and Tarzana Mental Health Clinic, to name two) and eventually to become a teacher and then Curriculum Coordinator in the L.A. County Jails, for twenty years.

My academic career really was launched from behind bars in the L.A. County Jails, even though I'd already worked in the L.A. Unified School district and in private schools as a substitute for several years.

During the preparation for this period of my life, I earned a Master of Arts degree, in English Literature and Speech from California State University, Northridge (I was always learning) and acquired a teaching credential in California, while also learning and practicing martial arts. Recently, I was inducted into the Martial Arts Masters Hall of Fame, and was given a Lifetime Achievement Award, but that's a little bit ahead of this introduction.

I may not have understood it fully at the time, but my success in various fields was mostly due to the fact that I was applying martial arts principles to whatever goal I set for myself, such as the completion of my Master of Arts thesis project analyzing the works of Carlos Castaneda from a literary perspective. I also applied the same principles when I was writing magazine and newspaper articles, or working in a jail or psychiatric hospital, creating and running a non-profit corporation, or even when I was learning to launch myself through the water faster than my competitors.

Later, I realized that five basic principles had guided me (as they had countless others before me) and I developed the *Go Tao Chi* or Five Principles of Chi, which I used to teach my Five Birds System. I have used these same principles for everything else I do, ever since.

The Five Birds System was first developed as a method of teaching martial arts concepts, regardless of the martial arts "style" that one favored. It had always annoyed me that, within a field where a "higher purpose" was at the core, there was a lot of infighting and backstabbing. I decided to remove myself from centuries old conflicts by focusing on the places where the styles agreed. This is how, in the Five Birds System, concepts became the focal point of the training. My goal was not only to teach people to punch and kick, but also to use their knowledge and skills to become better people and eventually good teachers of martial arts concepts in whatever endeavor that they used to define themselves. That is not an uncommon goal for a martial arts teacher and is supposed to be at the core of ALL martial arts training.

Where I differ however is that mine is a form that begins with the student. My goal as a teacher is to look for ways to make the lessons that I have to teach useful to the student. I believe that the value of any lesson is narrowly defined and that each student is unique. Therefore, each student must perceive and find value in the concepts from their own individual perspective. For this reason, I used to require my black belt candidates to bring their unique outlook into the school by contributing what we called a *special skill.* A special skill is defined as something that I do *not* teach each student, but one that they *bring to* the art. It was my way of helping them to see that what they were learning related to what others might perceive as outside interests. I've had students who used teaching as their special skill, or meditating, or computer programming, or snow skiing, or bike riding, or scuba diving, or healing practices, or trauma training, or edible plant collection, or any variety of professions and avocations. In many cases, a special skill led to a student following through by adopting that as their chosen profession. For example, many of my students have become teachers, doctors, managers etc. after having chosen a "special skill" that related to their future occupation. In all cases, I tried to find the shortest distance between the two points of their desire learn and what I had to teach. My teaching style was to try to distill lessons down into their essence and make a quick connection on as many levels as possible. So, no matter what subject I am teaching I always ask the student, ***"What is it that you need to accomplish?"***

Because of an unrestricted and broad view, I learned to apply what I call, a *saturation method* of teaching. This is a technique I named after observing my martial arts teachers, such as Bob Ozman, Mike Eaves, Frank Dux (and others). In this method, the concepts I touch upon encompass a great many disciplines and fitness regimens and I now strive to "teach the whole person" every lesson.

In my Five Birds System I use the symbols of the eagle, hawk, vulture, raven and owl to represent many different concepts, including 1) five basic strategies, 2) five styles of fighting, 4) the five powers, and 5) the five essential goals of a warrior.

I did not pick these concepts--or the birds that are represented in my hierarchy--out of thin air (pardon the pun), but witnessed these five birds, flying together (in actual air) during a ceremony that I was part of, many years ago. I was directed by my teachers to use the vision of these five birds, as a kind of focus for finding the path of my own life. It seemed like as good a model as any, and I've tried to stay true to this advice.

I realize now, through trial and error (one of the great life strategies of all time) that the pattern established by the momentary awareness that I call The Five Principles of Everything, are at the core of most martial arts training, but more so they are at the core of ALL the training that I've ever received. In other words, my teachers were only doing what they had learned from their teachers, and so on.

Another lesson that martial artists often use, and that has become apparent when studying everything else is, as we observe nature we can learn about ourselves. So, when observing the five birds, I saw that each can teach us something different, but each (though unique), also performs the simple but amazing task of flight.

All five of my birds are different, but in other words, because they are all birds of prey they also have similarities. By extension my teachers were also showing me that the concepts they taught (and the reasons we practiced) were not separate from nature, but part of it. In other words, the whole world seemed to be following similar rules and patterns that were admirable pathways for us to follow. Eventually, I understood what my teachers were truly trying to tell me. These patterns that were being revealed to me through both a mechanically stylized and naturally intuitive process were not just a blueprint that I had to follow, or that Nature followed, but also principles that the Universe seemed to follow.

The Five Principles that I developed originally related to body movement and merely simplified the study of martial arts by focusing on a relationship between movements and postures, or "the relation between ending and starting points." As with acupuncture, acupressure or a host of rituals or spiritual behaviors, Five Birds Martial Arts actions are performed in a specific way to achieve specific and non-specific benefits. This is also true of The Five Principles of Everything.

In this book, we will discuss how these principles can be applied to *your* special skill. We will start by telling you about the five basic principles, in general giving you examples of how they can be applied to virtually every endeavor. From health, to business, to politics, to social interactions, to any sport, profession or belief system the Five Principles are principles of EVERYTHING, because of the agreement that we share about them. A host of contributors and I will show you how these principles can be applied to narrow subjects such as writing, speaking, reading, teaching, running, dieting, business, swimming or self-defense or to broad topics like government, human relationships, health, economics or recovery from injury and disease. Often, by way of trying to make our points clear, we'll return to martial arts, because that is where I find my most familiar examples. I had one academic administrator suggest to me that I should "lose the reference to martial arts" in trying to explain the value of the Five Principles. I disagree.

Good martial arts teachers—My many contributors and I have found--are some of the best in the field of education, because they start from the premise that what they teach has applications beyond punching and kicking. I might add that I make this statement as someone who is known as much for his teaching skills, or writing skills, as for his martial arts skills.

Think about it. If you can teach people about life, about being better people, about the place of discipline, practice or perspective in achieving a happy life or about compassion, honesty, and truth while making them physically healthier, then perhaps you *have learned something of value*!

So, I will stick to the premise that what I present here is commonly understood in most martial arts practices. It is where I first learned of the commonality of the concepts, and therefore, I acknowledge martial arts teaching as the doorway, which revealed the application of these principles to all my other interests. Later in the articles and abstracts from experts in many other fields (some of these experts are also martial artists, first and foremost, as I am) you will get an opportunity to look at the simple premise of my thesis, from multiple perspectives.

To begin properly and simply, let me say that *in the language of martial arts, we say that Go-Tao-Chi (a fancy term I coined for The Five Principles of Everything) concentrates mainly on the relationship between Mind, Body and Spirit...or, if you prefer Awareness, Action and the Unknown.* In many formal lines of thought a "trinity" of these three ultimate powers is at the core of the philosophy.

In these same realms, the number five is also highly significant. I believe that the number five is thought important, partly due to the workings of the universe and partly because of humans own conceited ways of looking at things. After all, we DO have five fingers on each hand and five senses, don't we? This MUST be important, right?

Formerly, because I was most interested in martial arts, I used words to which my students related. For instance, the word *chi* in the broadest sense includes an understanding of the Japanese translation for the word *ki.* This word has multiple meanings, including *energy, life force, The Spirit, or "The Grand Ultimate"* (as it is usually translated in the exercise form of tai chi) among other things. These days I have changed my personal focus to network a broader perspective of the teachings. More and more I apply the Five Principles to the subject of communication, as I learn more about the power of words.

Recently, I published a novel entitled, *SHIDOSHI: The Four Ways of the Corpse.* It is a suspense-thriller that is based upon an ancient argument stemming from diverse translations to the first word in the title. In the fiction novel, I reference The Five Principles and infer that the corruption, conflicts and danger at the core of the suspense are all a result of not following the five principles.

Again, since my audience was made up primarily of martial artists, I used the phrase, Go-Tao-Chi to describe what I was doing. This is a term I coined from two separate languages (Japanese and Chinese). In the Japanese language the word *go* means both "hard" and the number "five." In the Chinese language, *tao* means, in one sense the *way*; or, it defines a set of circumstances to achieve certain goals. Chi is also a Chinese term that represents "life force" "energy" or "spirit." So, in what is intended as a *fully inclusive* translation Go-Tao-Chi means, *The Five Principles of Chi,* or *The Hard Principles of Chi.*

Unfortunately, because of my own diverse application of these principles, the original interpretation was too narrow for most people, because most are not interested in becoming martial arts teachers. However, if we broaden the scope of our observations (such as learning about five birds, instead of just one) we realize that the true test of these principles is their versatility. They are supposed to be applicable to everything, and purport to be the same set of rules that the Universe follows. If they cannot be applied to everything, then they are not applicable to anything, perhaps. That's the beauty of this system. Everything is boiled down to the observable five principles and ***the starting point is the consensus***, based upon the viewer's perspective.

The Five Principles of Everything are these: 1) The Principle of Applied Awareness, 2) The Principle of Flow, Action or Movement, 3) The Principle of Form 4) The Principle of Benefit and 5) The Principle of Harmony, Balance or Adaptability.

Being able to "put things in perspective" or to "see a pattern" seems to give us a sense of calm. Attention to these five principles, I believe will also allow one a sense of wellbeing (in a sense) in any pursuit where these principles are practiced and applied. At the end of the original Go-Tao-Chi book, I offered exercises for Five Birds Tai Chi practice as well as brief descriptions of how these exercises are used in several other of my special skills, established exercises or professional forms (Running, climbing, swimming, writing and teaching).

As an introduction to the articles section of this edition, Edward Tao (a former writing student of mine) has added a comment on how the principles are applied to tennis, as well as how he interprets the principles in translating to the Chinese language. In every abstract and article (including those by martial arts teachers) we are trying to show the diversity of the concepts and are merely giving these examples because they are areas where the individual writer has personal experience.

Let me make this very clear. ***No book or writing can ever be a substitute for personal experience***. We are not offering these principles as the ONLY ONES by which the Universe functions. They are simply patterns that appear to be observable by all and we do not oppose any other perspective, orientation, viewpoint or group, unless that viewpoint or group actively seeks to limit open, honest and individual inquiry.

Even within the *limited* realm of martial arts training, Go-Tao-Chi should NOT be considered a discipline unto itself. I taught Ninjitsu (a martial science taught to those who covet the title of ninja) for Frank Dux. Many people got caught up arguing about the validity of Ninjitsu, because they wrongly believed that it is taught as a particular style, with a limited number of techniques. That is not the case. The ninja used any technique that worked and suited the individual practitioner. That is how I developed Five Birds Martial Arts, how Frank Dux developed his FASST program (see his appendix at the end of this book) and how I teach and do everything today. Practical application of principles is at the core of every successful strategy and the reason why many of the contributors have requested to be a part of this book.

The Five Principles of Everything should be thought of as nothing more than a kind of blue print for general behavior. We should not, however get hung up on connotations when denotation is the goal. For example, on a purely physical level the tai chi postures and attention to relaxed movement (included in the original book) were intended to help the practitioner loosen the joints and reduce stress, while strengthening the tendons and toning the muscles. This was seen as an added benefit to the concepts and a way for me to deliver the message (since I needed to practice tai chi to be able to move properly). For this reason, I used tai chi, Yang Long Form movements as the basis.

However, Go-Tao-Chi (or Five Birds Tai Chi or Power Tai Chi, as it is sometimes called) is NOT really tai chi, for a couple of reasons. First, tai chi proper can only be considered in the cultural and historical context in which it was created. It was conceived in China by specific individuals and handed down in a familial context. In my case, for example I learned exercises that members of the Yang family had developed and passed from generation to generation. I also learned OTHER techniques that I incorporated into my workouts.

What I learned of tai chi was in the context of a bigger picture. It was never the ONLY picture and so much of what a tai chi student learns and practices, I simply don't know anything about. The important message is this: *Perspective is everything.*

Secondly, my Go-Tao-Chi concentrates on both ends of the energy spectrum (total relaxation and total tension). My concern is not only the *doing*, but also the *awareness* of the process. I often teach exercises that are NOT a part of any formal tai chi class, sometimes testing memory of a particular example from one class to the next, because paying attention to the instructor is what I'm trying to stress on that particular day. I do the same thing in a writing class.

Finally, since the philosophical foundations of Go-Tao-Chi *are* The Five Principles of Everything our goals are similar. We strive, in both, for *total fitness* through unity with all perspectives. Since, in the end, when I teach Five Birds Martial Arts or Five Birds Tai Chi, I often sway from the general precepts of Taoism and Zen to make points about concepts I am more concerned with, I don't feel comfortable claiming to be teaching tai chi. On the other hand, we must start someplace, and usually people have an idea of what they believe tai chi to be. So, I use that term or similar ones (such as The Meditation of Travel) to present the five principles from a place of familiarity, in the context that I wish to apply it.

With this said, I must add that many of my workshops and classes strongly emphasize physical health as a way to understanding something called ***total fitness***. This can be likened to right foundation coupled with right thinking and right action. However, there is one overriding physical principle for Go-Tao-Chi and that is: *For best results, all movements are relaxed and tension is only performed at correctly aligned, and stationary points*. This stems from the concept that each action, thought or driving force should have a purpose. In the case of The Five Principles, we ask, *"What is it you are trying to accomplish?"* Some people will respond, "self awareness," or "wellbeing" or "better health" Or even "self defense." Ultimately, we believe that having a clear picture of what you are trying to accomplish is paramount to success. Hence, the similarity of my movements to those in tai chi and the use of tai chi postures and movements in the practical description of concepts. However, don't be confused to believe that these concepts cannot be applied to your personal, specific interests. That is the whole point of creating this book. All of the contributors and I believe that these five principles can be applied to any endeavor. It is all a matter of emphasis and perspective. Therefore, we often refer to a particular discipline that absorbs our attention as "a meditation." What are we trying to accomplish with this nomenclature? The answer is *brevity.*

What makes something a meditation or an art? In the broadest sense, meditative movements can be ANY actions where the goal is total fitness and where the method of positive saturation is used at the level of body memory. In every discipline our goal is to take large amounts of information or big concepts and reduce them to bite-sized chunks.

By the way, there have been some very influential books of strategy in the past, which are now used as primers for life behavior. *The Book of Five Rings,* by Myamoto Mushashi, Sun Tzu's *The Art of War* are two examples that speak about "life and death" struggles by way of illustrating the relationship of all professions and all social structures to the idea of conflict. These two examples also use the number five as a memory device for their basic principles.

The goal of teaching the whole person (the individual) a specific thing (answering a question) to allow them to coexist in a group (understanding motivation, perspective and context) also seems to be important. For us, it is at the core of why we seldom justify an exercise with validation by authority. That means, that our system of teaching is not based upon what a particular master or expert said or what someone else told us. The concept's true import must be felt or experienced as an intuitively rediscovered truth to be of any real value. Our actions and thoughts are directed from and to the cells of the body and to and from the systems which control the way that the body functions.

Our goals in this book are basically very simple. At some level, concentrating on The Five Principles of Everything should help an individual experience their validity directly. All lessons are focused to that goal.

Whatever the subject I am teaching, if I realize that I'm not getting my point across in a class I change the lesson, not the student. In this way, the product grows naturally from the process of creating the form. In other words, the student's concepts of their individual goals hopefully merge with the teacher's goals at some point. It is the subtle difference between being a good parent and having the ability to procreate. Or, in martial arts terms it is the difference between being a black belt and a *sensei (*the Japanese word for a venerated teacher).

I said earlier that The Five Principles of Everything are like a blue print, because of the similarities (and differences) that a blue print has to the finished product. If you've ever had the experience of building a house from a blue print, or know anyone who has, you know that this document deals both with "general impressions" of what the house will look like, as well as the formal structural *requirements.* We can change the types of doors, the colors of paints and textures of the curtains, etc. We can even move the walls around to make the rooms bigger or smaller, or alter their shape. However, if we don't adhere to the basic requirements and building codes necessary for building a sound structure, we run the risk of the roof falling on our heads, the floor cracking or the windows and doors not closing properly.

On the other hand, the blue print of a house is NOT the house itself. It merely offers important information about the proper construction and successful completion of the project. By logical extension, a house is not, necessarily a home until it has been given "the personal touch." Every person who lives in the house will determine HOW the space is used, regardless of whether or not they've ever set eyes on the blueprint!

In my writing classes I tell my students that the primary purpose of any writing, speaking or reading is the same. The goal is communication. When we write (or read or speak) a sentence, paragraph, essay, speech, script or poem we are trying to say something (the voice) to someone (the audience). There are lots of different ways to accomplish this basic goal. There are many motivations for communication (from transmitting opinion to forming one, from giving information to concealing it). The way we choose to reveal or conceal is in itself communicating something. All forms of communication have some things in common. For instance, a sentence, a paragraph, a story or essay, all have prescribed requirements and suggested techniques that are based upon their and our similarities. In English, all have a beginning, a middle and an ending for instance.

Keeping this in mind, we emphasize that there are NO masters of the Five Principles of Everything, no black belts, no Phds or masters because, though the Five Principles can be thought of as a blueprint, they are never the houses. Each individual and individual "meditation, discipline or perspective" is the place where the principles dwell. Just as with any art, the "truth and beauty is in the eye of the beholder." Each person, master of their own domain, decides how to utilize the tools available to them.

The study and contemplation of these five universal principles form (and stem from) a Philosophy of Total Fitness, which strives to find common ground between all disciplines. That is why (as we go along) you will read how the five principles can be applied to a number of other kinds of exercises, philosophies, self-awareness programs, fitness regimens, business ventures, political views and academic courses of study.

The main method I use to teach this system is called *Concept Training*. In Concept Training we try to take complicated ideas and simplify them by concentrating on similarities rather than differences, as understanding and feeling relatedness are primary precepts to a successful life. In my martial arts classes, for example I have created "Maps" or pictures of complicated movements (like a dancer's step-map). In my writing classes I try to put complex lessons onto a single page, called Capsules where complicated ideas or longer lessons are reduced to the most basic forms. For many years I have been asking my writing (and martial arts) students to summarize their "rules of life" or "the most important lessons they've learned." My martial arts students know this as part of the "recapitulation" process where, for their black belt test they are asked to try and remember "every significant" moment and lesson throughout their lifetimes that led them to the moment when they felt they wanted to take their test. I got this term from the writings of Carlos Castaneda, who said that he learned it from a Yaqui Indian brujo named Don Juan Matus. Regardless, I've found the process to be a great way to organize and encapsulate each moment as a learning experience.

On my free website, Vision-Revision (and in many other localities), I've posted video clips from leaders and teachers of various disciplines, called their "Message in a Bottle." These messages are approximately two minutes in length videos where many celebrities "sum up" what they feel is the essential lesson that has shaped and molded them. In all cases, the Capsules, Messages, and Rules are a meeting point for clarifying complicated but important concepts such as "Know Thyself." Recent research into the workings of the brain reveals how important our preconceptions are in learning new material. In other words, if we expect to learn new and valuable things, we generally learn new and valuable things, but even this skill of optimism must sometimes be learned.

In addition, all martial artists begin their training with a belief that there is a close relationship between our physical self and the non-physical. The implication, of course is that there is an unseen part of us "out there" that can be experienced by the physical part, that there are two parts of each person. Generally speaking, however, we only feel these two parts of ourselves are separate until we gain some level of self-awareness at one, or the other level and then can integrate these "parts" into the concept of the whole.

Therefore, in martial arts, body movements are taught at the same time as concepts in the belief that while these two parts of our existence are somewhat separate, the proper attention given to one will benefit the other.

In communication we say that when one learns to read better, that skill will help their writing and speaking, and visa versa, and so on.

It is my experience that the easiest way to make the connection between an idea and what is felt, is by narrowing everything down to five basic concepts. ***The Five Principles of Everything help us to coordinate what we feel, think, believe and know with what we do.***

One final introductory note: This book is not intended to contain EVERYTHING that can be said or thought on the subjects that are used for illustration or even the concept of the Five Principles. Originally, my martial arts philosophy book was written like a poem and intended as *one way* of reinforcing what I taught in a class or on a video for self-defense on the subject of ***conflict avoidance***. I wanted to give my students a way to reinforce what they learned in a class and an opportunity to use the beauty and power of words as a stimulus for sincere reflection and to give myself an excuse for writing.

The purpose of this book (and the book's size) has grown with the demands. Therefore, what you see now is much more elaborate than what the first Five Birds Martial Arts students were given, but admittedly the examples are always those that deal with MY OWN INDIVIDUAL perspective and interests. I am a teacher/writer/martial artist, so naturally the science of education, philosophy of social interactions and the knowledge of the power of words are always paramount in my examples. Therefore, while this book continues to represent my own, best interests, it has become a source of interest and value to others who seek to organize their own Life Skills Strategy.

Remember, most of the lessons I apply here were given to me as a younger student and ignored until such time as I needed the information. The whole idea of "concept training" and Capsule Reviews or even putting everything into the Five Principles compartments came about because of my own strengths and weaknesses. I had a car accident that caused a concussion with neck and back injuries, for instance. These caused me to forget much of my training and prevented me from performing movements that at one time I thought were the pinnacle of the training. I am also a dyslexic who learned to read and love words according to my own methodology. The "maps" and "capsules" were just what I needed to relearn what I once took for granted.

In short, the teaching of The Five Principles of Everything has developed as I have developed into a better teacher and student, realizing that to be a true teacher is in itself a "higher calling." An important part of being a teacher at this level is that you understand you have responsibilities in every dynamic. Remember that everyone can learn from every other person. To impart what you know "for the benefit of the student," turns teaching into a much more noble adventure; just as, becoming an elected official "for the sake of the constituency" turns politics into the kind of calling that men like John Adams or Thomas Jefferson envisioned it to be. Also, it's important to understand the *motivations* of those who become your students, regardless of how brief a moment that arrangement might span. Here is something else I've learned to be very valuable: *some students understand best through the written word, while others have a tendency toward other modes of learning.*

Every good teacher or student knows that lessons are best learned on multiple levels. One modality does not replace another, but simply enhances it, by offering another perspective. Finally, I believe that The Five Principles of Everything are represented, in part, by our behaviors. For this reason, the student-teacher (or parent-child, employer-employee, citizen-representative, merchant-customer, provider-beneficiary) relationship is part of the natural flow of life, and so are our socialization skills.

Therefore, even though the ultimate goals are very much personal in nature, group classes do play an important role. Communication and interaction are basic human needs. The more classes one attends (both group and private) and serious private speculation, in which one engages, will ultimately produce a special relationship with the Principles in this book. Also, it doesn't hurt to offer awards and incentives (appropriate to each individual) along the way. In other words...the three secrets to making the Five Principles of Everything a valuable part of your specific life are the same as those for everything else...Practice, Practice and Practice.

Now, let's get right to the five principles and how they relate to one another, following another piece of advice that has been echoed throughout literature, "It's always best to start at the beginning."

"The Five Birds in the Five Bird System are identified as The Eagle, The Hawk, the Vulture, The Raven and the Owl. The Five Goals of a Warrior (that these birds, partially, represent) are Spirit, Honor, Courage, Skill and Adaptability. All these birds represent different paths to the same place. We observe them, trying NOT to copy their behavior, but to uncover where their behavior is like our own and what bird reflects our natural tendencies."

—GFR

Chapter One

THE PRINCIPLE OF APPLIED AWARENESS

A simple definition of this first principle is: ***The way we think and feel about something affects the outcome of our actions.*** This may seem rather obvious to many of you, and, that is good. We believe that the truth of any subject is often obvious and can be verified intuitively. In fact, one test of whether something is truly beneficial is whether or not it can be stated simply. What good is a truth that is so complicated that we can never understand nor express it, and can not trust our own feelings about its validity?

In fact, it appears that as human beings, one of our fundamental functions is to become more aware and to unravel the mysteries of our awareness. If someone or some organization says that already have a lock on the only true awareness of truth, or they are trying to keep secrets or to interfere with our natural desire to know, then that organization should be suspect.

Albert Einstein basically said that the purpose of all science is to give us a glimpse of the workings of the universe. Science, art and spiritual truth (martial or otherwise) do not contradict one another. Uncovering truth and finding answers to a continual array of questions is what we are all about.

Human beings are ultimately attuned to the fact that "life as we know it" is directly related to the concept of Applied Awareness. We exalt facts or data or applied skills to the extent that we award degrees and high paying jobs to those who "know" more than others or can use their knowledge to a mutually beneficial end.

However, facts are not awareness. Our ability to *apply* what we've learned, to prove it, to demonstrate what we feel to be true is also part of the basic building blocks of success. This is why the principle of Awareness, is often referred to as The Principle of *Applied Awareness*.

This initial principle stems from the belief that awareness, in its many forms (a multi-layered awareness), is what sets human beings apart from other creatures on planet Earth. Our abilities to perceive the world around us, to be aware (both self aware and sensitive to our surrounding environment and related systems and creatures) to analyze and to think creatively, to intend, to will, to predict and to focus our attention are all at the core of what we are.

Awareness can be thought of as both the vehicle and the fuel of our existence. It can be both externally directed and internally applied. Awareness makes us wonder what is beyond the next hill, and then it motivates us to go and look over that hill to the next horizon. When we get to the place we were heading, we pit the information we gathered along our journey against our preconceptions to measure the value of where we are. In Zen koan fashion, I sum it up this way: *Look where you are. See where you are going and remember where you've been.*

Awareness is an essential element in achieving true happiness, since the idea of being unaware that we are happy leaves something to be desired. We could say, in short, that for many of us human beings, Awareness Is Everything.

There are, of course, many levels and applications of this one principle. It might be said that things like thinking, arguing, praying, wishing, questioning, believing and knowing as well as meditating caring, sympathizing, empathizing, understanding and wondering are all levels of Applied Awareness.

Rather than define the differences of each of these levels here, let's emphasize the agreed upon “truth” and say that any area of inquiry must begin with an application of awareness and that workshops in all endeavors are conducted specifically for this purpose.

There are a couple of points that bear repeating, since the ability to "trade strategies" or to say the same thing in various ways, is a basic tool of Concept Training. Most importantly: Concept Training springs directly from an acceptance of The Principle of Applied Awareness.

Keeping sight of goals

This first principle of everything implies that humans are goal oriented. Believe it or not, people have argued endlessly with me about that point, and I was forced to say to them, as I say now, ***if you have a problem with that statement then utilizing The Five Principles of Everything is not for you.***

On the other hand, if you can accept that humans are goal oriented, then one of the things that will help you succeed in achieving your goals is to have a clear picture of what it is you are trying to accomplish. The clearer the picture we have of our attempted accomplishments, the more likely we will be able to achieve them. In fact, this first principle is an easy place to check for flaws in any system or belief. One of the first questions I always ask in a brainstorming or consulting session is: What are you trying to accomplish? What is your goal? Even in the initial stages of open-ended, theoretical research project, where information is gathered but its importance is not yet understood, there is always categories and methods for organizing what we learn. In writing and business, this stage is often referred to as brainstorming.

Later we will talk about the other principles of everything, such as finding the best form of expression and how the concept of motion is engrained in our systems. Within each of these however, it is important to remember that the five principles are always all-inclusive. Concentrating ONLY on one principle or (more seriously) believing that an individual principle is the goal itself is a mistake. When we examine forms for flow or benefit we must also apply a proper attitude. In other words, no single interpretation of a principle can be deemed “correct” unless it does not violate any of the other principles. So, if our goal, for instance is merely to “prevent someone else from exercising their freedoms” then that is a violation of the basic principles. Or, more simply, if we decide that our goal is to interfere with someone else's goal, then that should be a red flag that problems are inherent in our form. If one department’s success is dependent on another’s failure, then the business plan is faulty. Okay?

Keeping sight of our goal is one application of Applied Awareness that we can easily measure for ourselves. If we are scattered, or if we change course (side-tracked without purpose) in the middle of an activity, we might never accomplish anything, and accomplishments is often a measure of the value of a lifetime. Trying to follow the five principles in everything that we do is not a specific activity, though. It is rather a way of looking at what we do as a way of finding patterns in successful behavior and measuring our own behavior against those patterns.

The starting point in this quest is the knowledge that each person is unique and learns differently. People exercise (or avoid it) for instance, for different reasons. They have different body types, strong points and weaknesses. A person might study martial arts for a number of reasons, too (from self defense to self awareness). The Five Principle approach not only respects the individual, but also asks the individual to acknowledge their uniqueness.

An adherence to the Five Principles of Everything, offers a method for taking a step back, and distilling what we are observing by asking one all important question: What is my goal? Or: Is what I'm doing helping me to achieve my goal without violating the other principles? If you keep this in mind, then you may well be using The Five Principles to make your profession or avocation, or indeed every thought and activity conform to a meditative (and therefore) natural, human process. Always, it is better to make what is natural "work for us" rather than fight against the stream of our inbred tendencies.

Taking Responsibility

Taking Responsibility is another level of Applied Awareness that needs to be more fully discussed. When we accept responsibility for our actions, our choices and even our feelings this add a level of immediacy to our lives, forcing us to live in the *now* of our thoughts, deeds and emotions. For this reason, following the Five Principles exalts the value of the individual as they relate to the big picture, and encourages each person to look for patterns that reveal how ones actions, thoughts and feelings are in keeping with universal ones.

Compare those who feel negatively about *exercise* or *diet* to those who are completely immersed in exactly the same activities, but have framed their chosen way of thinking, as a positive experience rather than a task and you will have a measure about the advantage of thinking in terms of applied awareness.

There are many stories of those who say that they hate math, writing or hate exercising in general for examples. So, instead of forcing a student to perform specific tasks--which the student might know to be beneficial, but still think and feel so negatively about--a good teacher will try to divert their attention onto another activity which they will accept in a better light. In today's educational jargon, this is called "contextualized learning."

For instance, instead of running, a teacher might take students tracking, herbal plant gathering, or instruct them in the mediation of motion (a general topic). As they learn about various animals or wild plants they are also being taught about running as a form of meditation, hooking their minds on a number of related tasks.

In this way, breathing, visualization, hand positioning, focusing the eyes, listening to the sounds of running, land-tracking, exploring for gold or learning about the weather might help to teach the BODY and the MIND separately, but on the same subjects and without the perceived negative baggage. There are so many interesting details in each of these activities and concepts to consider that one does not notice the isolated fact that they are running, or maybe just walking which are both, of themselves very healthy objectives.

In other words, from a Five Principles perspective we never recommend someone do anything for *exercise*. However, we often suggest that a person run (or something like it), because that is a natural expression of movement and may be necessary for the task in which you're engaged. Aerobic exercise, on a purely physical level, is known to be valuable for overall health! If your goal is overall health, then aerobic activity is an important ingredient. People who say that they hate running or *can't stand the idea of running*, will usually end up *tracking*, or *gathering plants* for hours...covering great distances and getting the aerobic exercise that they need to maintain good physical health. Ultimately, that is what we are really trying to accomplish. How we get there, is not important. The idea of *no pain, no gain* is therefore flawed at its core. We know that awareness, if applied properly is always beneficial. Pain, very well may be a way for the body to protect itself from further injury. Pain, from the Five Principle perspective is an awareness that helps one avoid more and greater, unnecessary pains or ills.

It is also important not to get caught up in one of the nuances of a general goal. To illustrate this, let's look at the general subject of Education. In the *olden days* (I use that term with my younger students to define any time before NOW or a time before any individual becomes particularly self-aware) it used to be that students found teachers who could teach them a particular "system or pattern" so that the student could one day use that awareness, knowledge or skill to integrate into society. Some people became academics, others physical laborers and within each of these strata there were various divisions, skill sets, and specialties. If a student found a teacher who taught them something that they did not find useful, that student either found a different teacher or was miserable in their station in life and cursed the drudgery of their existence. In any case, within the general concept of education, learning and the student must remain the primary focus. The student-teacher dynamic was a big part of the success or failure of the individual to achieve their goals. Everyone who had a clear understanding of the process of learning and the ultimate goal of education (in general), and adhered to the patterns that had been established through trial and error, were the ones who most likely would benefit from the system.

Today, we hear a lot of people (individuals, groups and organizations) declare that they are *educators*, that their primary goal is education. We have federal, state, county, city, regulators, boards, czars, unions and bureaucracies whose primary functions are to establish measurements and structures and rules for learning. There is nothing wrong with having structures or rules or even bureaucracies as long as they can honestly answer the questions, "What is it you are really trying to accomplish?" and "Is that goal consistent with ALL of the Five Principles?" This means, that every nuanced system needs to be directed toward the same goal if they are truly part of the same thing. It is, for example why good and successful structures usually have a mission statement that is a clear and concise summary of where the organization wants to focus their awareness.

The truth is that the individuals who are most important in the equation of "how do we best accomplish education?" are the students themselves and to a slightly lesser degree, the teachers. School boards are not fundamentally interested in education, nor are unions. School boards are interested in the fiduciary responsibilities of running a district. Teacher Unions have been created to protect teachers. There is nothing wrong with either of these two groups or their goals, but school board members and union representatives should not call themselves educators, unless everything they are doing is for that purpose.

Teachers and the students themselves are the only primaries in the educational process. Even within a single subject we see how important it is to "keep sight of the goal." To teach or learn science, for instance requires certain skills, tools and mindsets. One should not have to take into account some arbitrary measuring stick that has nothing to do with a particular subject of inquiry because an outside bureaucracy is trying to force their goals or even point of reference into the equation.

In all cases, how we think about something determines, in part, the result we achieve. We've heard it said that to achieve we have to conceive and believe. The beauty of testing this theory with our own bodies is that we can feel the results, as well as understand them.

In self-defense classes we learn various techniques that our teachers once learned from their teachers, or were created by our teachers based upon what they could assimilate of their teacher's lessons. Whenever I observe a martial arts class and I hear an instructor say, “My teacher used to do it this way, but I do it differently because…” or tell a woman or child to vary a technique because they have a different set of strengths and weaknesses from the adult male students, then I know that that lesson is based upon a sincere desire to teach and therefore an understanding of the Five Principles.

That teacher knows that their student's objectives, skills or physical abilities may be vastly different from those of the master. Some people learn martial arts, not to ever defend themselves or even for combat purposes or to earn titles or certificates. Some people are just trying to get a good workout. That's the reason why we have sport karate, MMA, traditional styles and even true combat styles that are taught only to police and military. Many people start martial arts classes with only a vague idea of what they want to accomplish (they brainstorm the concept of martial arts). Everybody is punching and kicking for different reasons. Many martial arts schools are run by teachers who begin by offering what they believe is a traditional product, but end up struggling to keep their heads above water, financially by selling other products or services. Each should understand "what it is they are really trying to accomplish" from the beginning and use it as a point of reference, proceeding from there. Certainly, our goals change as we change and grow. A martial arts student might try classes for one reason, but remain in them for quite a different reason altogether. A student in college may have one major course of study at the beginning of their academic careers, but end up pursuing a wholly different profession in the end. Or, maybe the degree or certificate they end up with will have nothing more to do with the rest of their life besides proving to others (or themselves) that they are not quitters. That is part of the fifth principle of everything that we will discuss in a later section.

For now, let us say that awareness is a two-way street. We become aware, and our awareness can be focused to enhance results. As you become more familiar and relaxed with The Five Principles you can test this, too, for yourself by simply concentrating your awareness on different parts of the body. Then, with practice, you will be able to associate the various techniques, methods, systems and applications with general feelings of wellbeing, health and relaxation or even increased energy, or pain reduction. The beauty of this way of thinking is that each of us gets to decide. Each of us gets to take responsibility.

Trust Yourself

The ability to trust oneself is another famous motivational concept that is really only a nuanced variation of the Applied Awareness principle. It is well known that self-doubt practically guarantees failure. When we judge everything by the Five Principles the individual's experience (and their interpretation of success) is paramount. It is also implied that the only true test of something's value is how it relates to the individual. Beware of falling into a dangerous trap! Open, honest and educated evaluation is far different than blind and ignorant trust. There are many examples of gurus and other well-spoken leaders guiding vast numbers of people down the wrong road.

I wrote my Master of Arts in English Literature thesis on the works of Carlos Castaneda, for example. My focus was the impact of his writing and the beauty of some of the concepts expressed in the works from a literary perspective.

Many individuals followed Castaneda's teachings to the letter (reportedly from an elder master named Juan Matus, who received these teachings from previous instructors, etc.) that were handed down, Castaneda said, from a period in antiquity for the express purpose of allowing Castaneda and his few close associates enough "power" to break the shackles of humanness and *defy death*. Sound familiar?

Many of the techniques that Castaneda taught were contrary to the Five Principles that we are discussing here, and his followers did not ask simply, "What am I trying to accomplish by my own behavior?" When Carlos Castaneda died, many of his followers were left with a feeling of emptiness and shame based on the belief that they had wasted years of their lives following a false prophet. These sad souls completely rejected any truth that was in the books. Some however, took what was good and useful in Castaneda's teachings and created their own patterns that did not violate any of the Five Principles. In other words, when a follower becomes a teacher and takes responsibility for that new role, then they have achieved enlightenment. This usually turns out well for everyone, including and most importantly the students themselves.

Beginner's Luck

You've probably experienced Beginner's Luck at some point in your life. You try something for the first time and are successful, but then, upon learning more about the accomplishment, you are unable to achieve the same results. Some people believe that all beginners are just luckier that others and that failure (with practice) will inevitably follow. Others believe that beginners often succeed because they trust their teachers and because of this they do not have a clear picture of failure. I recall learning to play golf from my father at the age of ten. Without any direction my dad put a ball on the tee and told me to whack it with the club he was handing me, toward the flag that I could see in the distance.

I did as instructed and the ball landed about two feet from the cup. When we walked up to the green, I saw the hole where the flag was placed and my dad told me to push it with another club (the putter) into the hole. I did as directed, not realizing that I had just scored what my father called "an eagle." His face lit up, obviously thinking that he had a golf prodigy on his hands and he began to teach me how to hold the club, how to interlock my fingers and align my thumbs, how to stand, how to hold my head, swing the club in a circle etc. I have never been able to recreate that initial success and do not enjoy the game of golf, at all.

That carefree, innocence is the framework from which all our actions must be accomplished. "Child is Father To the Man," is a Judeo-Christian phrase that deals with this. Understand the meaning of Applied Awareness in this light, and you are well on your way to utilizing the First Principle of Everything.

One martial arts game that I created I call Catch the Rabbit. This fun exercise utilizes several small beanbags that are simultaneously thrown and caught with both hands. Each bag is weighted and filled differently. One has beans and five pounds of steel shot. Another has large wooden balls added to the beans. A third usually has some sort of inner lining that causes the bag to "jump" out of ones hands (hence the name), and so on. While each bag looks and "sounds" the same, each must be caught and thrown differently because of their differences in weight and filling. The game requires that each person pay attention to both the throwing and catching applying equal importance to each, and participants are told that, in general, one is learning to block and punch with this exercise. Adults often have reservations about catching one bag, let alone several in a continuous routine of throws and catches that looks like team juggling to everyone involved. Kids never hesitate to play the game with joy, but both adult and child are forced to succeed because there are too many bags coming at them to concentrate on failure. What they are NOT being told is that they are learning the difference between focusing their awareness and expanding it, at the same time. How is this message delivered? After a short amount of success, throwing and catching accurately with both hands (something that most adults say they cannot do before beginning) the student is asked, "At what point do you decide HOW you are going to catch each bag?"

You see, because of the different weights and fills of the bags, they must be caught and thrown differently as well. So, when does this decision take place? The answer is: *at the moment of contact*. The heavy, shot-filled bag must be allowed to "come to you," while the "rabbit" must be grabbed quickly with the fingertips. If the rabbit is allowed to hit the palm, it will jump out and land on the floor. The one with the giant wooden balls must also be treated differently, as it cannot be grabbed (except precisely on one ball) or allowed to "come to you" as it too will pop out of your palm. So, while you are concentrating on throwing the bags precisely (also different with each bag), you are making decisions about the catch. To succeed you must also expand your awareness to take into your perception all the bags, coming and going at the same time (in both the left and right hands), while focusing your awareness on each individual bag, catching and throwing. It is a great way to "see and feel" how, indeed awareness can be internally directed and externally directed, expanded and focused simultaneously. It's one of the best ways I've ever found to teach this important lesson. Every good businessperson knows that details and the big picture must be kept in view at all times to achieve success. In meditation, an awareness of this concept sometimes takes years of practice. When they have achieved this level of awareness it is said they have glimpsed nirvana.

An individual can be also taught to catch one of my beanbags blindfolded, in just a few minutes! Naturally, when you tell a child that they are going to learn to catch a bag blindfolded, they are usually anxious for the opportunity. Adults, with preconceptions of failure, are often harder to convince, but in all of the decades that I've been teaching, I have yet to fail on the first try to teach *anyone* how to accomplish this amazing task. Come to a Five Principles seminar some time, and one of my certified instructors or I will show you how to do it.

A Positive Attitude

A positive attitude is something that you might have been born with. Others must develop it. There are numerous books and techniques for increasing and reinforcing a positive self-image. Here, let us say that regardless of whether you feel you were born with a positive disposition or just struggle for it, utilization of The Five Principles happens both externally and internally and that a positive attitude is a nuance of Applied Awareness that certainly can help.

Another important point is this: The principles can be seen to work from the inside out and the outside in at the same time. Give yourself, at least the opportunity to develop a positive attitude, by affirming that the possibility exists.

In most twelve step recovery programs we hear the phrase "expect a miracle." The phrase to remember here might be, "Always start from a positive perspective." Obstacles will always present themselves in different ways to different people, but focusing ONLY on the obstacles is a dead end street, since this is appears to be a violation of the basic principle of awareness that the forces of life operate upon.

The more you work in this way, the more you will benefit IN BOTH DIRECTIONS. The more you benefit, the less you will have to work. Practice all your lessons as if they are of utmost importance, with the attitude that you will benefit and you have set yourself in the center of the river of success. All you must do now is watch for obstacles and let the river carry you. Remember, it is believed that how we think and problem solve, indeed that we problem solve at all, is not only an indication of our humanness, but our innate desire to cooperate with "how things are." Whenever a student asks me if the future will be better or worse than the present, I don't hesitate to respond, "Better!" Not only does it appear that optimism is better than pessimism, but solving problems is what we do as a species. In essence, the desire to make things better is inbred in each of us.

Paying attention

In the Five Principles perspective it is assumed that there are degrees of concentration. The better you are able to concentrate—these days we know this by another term introduced by Carlos Castaneda: *intending*) the greater the result. We also believe that our attention can be focused to specific parts of our body, or specific tasks so that benefits can be personalized, in a sense, to meet the individual's needs. Becoming willing to pay attention to each other, oneself, or to a narrow aspect of any system are in themselves valuable objectives. Everything takes practice, including failure. If we practice (think, act or feel) negatively, then the result is likely to be negative. Many teachers emphasize practicing, "perfectly." For most of us, the road to perfection often begins with honestly, willingly and openly concentrating on the starting point.

One exercise for experiencing "controlled awareness" or "becoming aware of your mind, body spirit connection" is to tense and relax an isolated part of your body...one hand, for instance. Continue tensing and relaxing until the isolated body part becomes tired and begins to tingle or burn. Suddenly, relax that part of your body and turn your attention to another part...the other hand, in this case. Try to transfer the feeling that you had in the hand you tensed to the other hand that has not been in your attention, just by looking at it or concentrating on it.

You will see that you will easily be able to duplicate the tingling feeling in the other part of your body just by thinking about it. More amazingly, the hand that was once tired will be forgotten, often feeling as if it had never moved!

Self-Awareness and A Second Attention

The five principles of everything appear to have a purpose in the universe that is parallel to your own individual bodies. Therefore, we both seem to strive to heighten awareness at more than one level. However, if we had to narrow all the many ways down to their opposites, we would have to say that we strive for Self Awareness (the ability to focus awareness internally) and a heightened awareness of the world around us (the ability to expand awareness externally). When we achieve an understanding of this duality, we call the heightened awareness a Second Attention, which is a whole new way of concentrating on more than one task or movement or concept simultaneously with another *but with a common purpose*. The term "second attention," was also introduced in the writings of Carlos Castaneda, but he did not create the concept. In the now famous *Book of Five Rings*, by Miyamoto Musashi, we learn of a state of being that is "Open At All Eight Corners." Musashi was a 15th century, Japanese sword-master. His Book of Five Rings is a reading primer for American businesspeople today, to learn how the mind of a Japanese businessperson works. Musashi told us that he taught and practiced sword fighting, not as a way to defeat an opponent in battle, but to "become aware" of this new way of viewing life. Another martial text from Okinawa (in about the same period), known as the *Bubishi* measures success in something referred to as *mushin*, or no mind.

We say today that our pursuit of the indescribable essence of life starts from the act of controlled awareness, or paying attention. Musashi emphasized that what he learned from the life and death struggles of sword fighting, could be applied to any endeavor. He wanted his students to understand only five principles or concepts. He emphasized that if one fought with a sword, one should be of the single-mindedness that “there are no blocks, only cuts.” To Musashi, it was essential that his students understand that “what it was that they were trying to accomplish” was to cut their opponent. Everything he said and did was for that purpose. There was no reason to block your opponent’s sword because the sword, by itself, was not a danger. The person holding the sword was the opponent. Therefore there was no movement that was not focused on cutting the other person.

Musashi also introduced a completely new concept in Samurai culture and that was to use both swords at the same time. He created the “niton ichi ryu” or “two swords as one” style. Whereas other Samurai used only their katana for fighting, while keeping the short, suicide sword in their belt, Musashi filled both hands with cutting weapons. “If you have two swords, you should use two swords” was his logic. This 2-to-1 advantage and single-minded focus made him legendary. He was supposedly unbeatable.

From an acceptance of the Principle of Applied Awareness, knowledge of yourself and others develops to almost a power unto itself. Though knowledge is NOT really power, any knowledge CAN increase your options. You never know when a seemingly insignificant piece of information will come in handy.

"For me there is only the traveling on paths that have heart, on any path that may have heart. There I travel, and the only worthwhile challenge is to traverse its full length. And, there I travel, looking, looking, breathlessly."

—Don Juan Matus, From Carlos Castaneda's

The Teachings Of Don Juan

Chapter Two

THE PRINCIPLE OF FLOW,

Motion or Action

A simple explanation of how we utilize this principle is to state simply (after accepting that energy exists) that energy (and all its representations) moves or flows. As with all the basic principles there are subtle shades of meaning, as well as numerous applications. The Principle of Flow is no exception. With the Principle of Flow we are saying, "Energy favors motion; Therefore, all strategies, plans, equations and theories that are worth our effort...take (or have an awareness of) the movement of something (even time)." As this relates to Awareness, we can say that information is most valuable when we put it to use.

One important variation on this theme can be seen in the questions, "What moves us? What motivates our actions? Or even, how does my personal strategy motivate or stir emotion in others?" All these questions are ones that Aristotle may have asked, and we are still asking them. Why? It is because these questions are grounded in the same five principles that are at the core of human development.

Because we are human, we feel a need to try to establish a prioritized value to our actions. With the Principle of Flow, we will begin our discussion about the application of this awareness by asking first how, or why energy or flows. It's important to note that answering the question of "why?" is not essential to a feeling of satisfaction or happiness, but asking the question seems to be an important part of being human, as it is part of the process of gathering information or gaining awareness.

To prove that the Principle of Flow applies to all strategies, we must begin with the simple acceptance that chi, or energy, or our life essence (whatever you want to call it) does, indeed exist.

Some people believe that we cannot prove the existence of a life force with scientific methods. That is not our main purpose here (it is one of those side-roads we talked about earlier). However, we believe that there are many such scientific proofs of an energy that is called *chi* by the Chinese and *ki* by the Japanese. Proof, however is not important if it has no strength in an individual's life. That is a common debate tactic, to segue an argument that you feel you're losing, to something else that is unrelated (common in today's political arena especially). In this case, we don't want to prove anything other than our original premise that there are principle commonalities in all successful strategies and systems. The one that we are discussing here, we call the Principle of Flow.

If you cannot agree that you are alive OR that all the examples of energy that we can witness (electric current, even movement within an atom) do tend to show that the universe is in motion, then you should probably quit here. In addition, I will say that, just as Awareness can be defined on many levels, Flow can also be multi-layered. Emotion, for instance, is a word that means, literally, "In Motion." Usually, people don't think of their feelings as being tangible NOR moving...but this aspect of humanity also follows the same basic rules of movement.

So, we'll proceed on the assumption that we can experience energy (call it what you will) within our own bodies (if nothing else) and that what we experience will indeed prove that it FLOWS. For now, let us simplify even further and say, "In the development of a life strategy, The Principle of Flow is everything." Again, however let's take a look at the many variations and shades of application and add that "the rate of flow" is also very important.

Albert Einstein's famous equation E=MC2-translated to mean that Energy can be converted to physical matter when (and if) the mass is moved at the speed of light/squared. This magical equation (demonstrating that mathematics is our common language with the universe itself) basically shows us that the amount of energy that is apparent, is directly related to speed and time. One less dramatic illustration of this in our immediate, human world can be seen in a bullet. If you take a small piece of lead and throw it at something, there will likely be little result. However, if you take that same bit of lead, put a charge of gunpowder behind it and get it moving really fast…well, you can see the relationship. Varying the rate of flow can change the same basic movement from a loving pat to an aggressive strike.

When humans try to make sense of abstracts, we often look to Nature or our own bodies—to the concrete and observable—to glimpse the ultimate truths. Where else are we to go for reliable verifications? Therefore, by way of explaining further the Principle of Flow, let's look at the simple act of breathing. At the beginning of this book we quote a Zen proverb that states, "*The Universe Breathes both Hard And Soft*." This proverb is a basis for the practice of some types of martial arts and also why a study of only one way of doing something often seems lacking. For instance, tai chi emphasizes relaxed and slow movements.

Let me say here that Tai Chi (again, you can insert ANY specific field of study or discipline here) is ALL THAT

SOME PEOPLE NEED to gain their ultimate goals or to grasp all the principles of everything. I am not one of those people, however. On the other hand, I have always favored a multi-layered approach. Perhaps I am just hardheaded, but I need to have my lessons on grand scale and many levels for me to understand them. Sometimes it takes years (or even decades) for me to realize the significance in the value of lessons that are offered to me or even my own words. Many times I've heard people echo this sentiment by lamenting, "I wish I'd listened to my own advice."

We've heard the saying, "Wisdom comes with age." This saying implies that, over time, a level of understanding (our ultimate goal as humans) will be achieved where we are satisfied. This also points to the fact that a variation of speed, and an allowance for "slowing things down" or even changing direction, might be necessary to achieve a certain goal.

I like to swim and to run as meditative practices and I used to spar (or fake fight). Naturally, these activities are beneficial as aerobic activities. We're told by medical people that if we get our hearts pumping at a fast rate for a period of time, that this is a good thing.

I experienced a car accident and was unable to do the some of the things that I most relied upon for general health.

I felt completely frustrated and basically gave up. I knew that I needed to move to be happy, but I did not remember the most important part of my teachers' lesson in this regard. It took years before I realized that I could move "differently" according to the new set of circumstances where I found myself. I started practicing tai chi, a moving meditation (martial arts techniques) that expressly suggests that "slow is best." I then applied this same concept to running and swimming, realizing that (as I'd always said), "Anything is better than nothing." I started to feel better, even though I could not move at the same pace as I did before the accident, because I was back applying all five principles to my life, as best I could. I made progress.

Today, I often go for a run, never getting above a fast walk, and spending more time "stopping to smell the flowers" or gazing at the ocean than I do actually putting one foot in front of the other. I keep in mind what it is that I really want to accomplish by the activity I call running. An outside observer might have a totally different term for what they perceive I am doing. Regardless of the term, the Principle of Flow is present.

Even when I was in the best of shape, I knew that the form of running had many possible variations. For instance, one can be a sprinter or a long-distance runner. Running on dirt is very different than running on asphalt, concrete or a track. Cross country running-sometimes known as off road running-cannot generally be compared for speed to track events, but generally, the unpredictability of the terrain is what makes it interesting to the participant. One usually experiences uphills and downhills during a cross country run, and must adjust the pace, stride and even the equipment that is used accordingly unless of course the location of the run is the beach. Then the tides must be taken into account, or other variables that relate to flow. In the mountains, one never runs down in quite the same way as they run up. Of course, walking, trekking, jogging, hiking and even climbing all have similar but different specific details that must be considered. Yet, all are essentially moving ones body across the surface of the earth.

Looking back at the car accident itself, it must be considered that Einstein's equation played a big part. The injury caused by the mass and speed of the car that hit me was compounded by the fact that my body was completely at rest and then awkwardly set into motion, albeit only briefly. I probably felt the effects, not only of this one "hit" but also of the accumulated strikes that my body had endured over the course of decades. The proverbial *straw that broke the camel's* back must be placed there to do the damage. Indeed, the awareness that can be applied to either running, or to my car accident in the bigger picture of my life in general, is dependent not only upon the applications of ideas, but of the interaction between and violation of the basic principles of form, benefit and flow. In this way, we see that a successful strategy (one where there is a definite and definable benefit) relies on the interplay *between* the principles and not specifically in any one of them.

There are others who feel that The Five Principle approach to problem-solving picks up, for them, where other strategies leave off. Even in Five Birds Martial Arts classes, however, we stress that ANY activity that combines mind, body and spirit and leads one to the ultimate goal of awareness can be considered a meditative form. Musashi admitted that he was putting his life strategy into sword fighting terms because he knew about sword fighting. However, he also taught his students to be as knowledgeable as possible "in all professions." Sun Tzu spoke of the classes of warriors, and even the principles themselves as they related to each other. Nothing was more significant than anything else.

This non-judgmental approach is, I believe, essential in the development of a successful life strategy, because, a student must be able to see the relationship of ANY point of reference to any OTHER point of reference. They cannot be bound. They must be allowed to move freely. However, if they decide to be still, that too is o.k. and a representation of the principle of flow.

A good teacher is one who seeks to understand the multiple perspectives of his/her students and then establishes the core curriculum as the "main objective" of the course of study. Each student needs to know "where he or she is going" and about how long it is going to take to get there. There are some forms of meditation (and associated rituals) or fields of study (and associated lessons) that focus entirely on the concept of flow (and don't forget the popular motorcycle add that proclaimed, "It's not the destination, but the journey").

Some images that are often repeated in the teaching and discussion of Flow are: The Circle (or cycle) of Life...and Death—The River of Life, The Road or Path of Life—the idea of infinity or life without end, the continual flow of opposite forces as with the symbol of yin and yang. These are all based upon natural, human considerations and observations. They all also show the relationship of three things: The Known, The Unknown, and the (currently) Unknowable.

We can say that what we know is that on which we base our physical actions. What is Unknown, is currently beyond our consideration, may have immediate perceivable results at a known level, and as conditions change, may well become known. The Unknowable is beyond our grasp (from our current perspective). We cannot perceive directly the Unknowable; we can only sense its essence when it touches us, indirectly, through what is known and unknown. It is O.K. to wonder and ask the question "Why?" but NOT when we think that the question itself is our ultimate pursuit as humans. There must always be balance!

"Energy can neither be created nor destroyed." —Albert Einstein

The concept of Flow can lead to complicated philosophical questions, but in the end, with sustained flow, a subtle acknowledgement of the constant flux between the Known, the Unknown and the Unknowable is achieved. This limited awareness of chi/energy/awareness is all we can ever hope to accomplish.

Remember, "Energy favors motion." However, movement (or learning, or enlightenment) can come at different speeds, sometimes almost imperceptibly. So, ones NEED or desire to know can often precede their wisdom or ability to utilize the awareness, but gathering information and then making decisions based upon our observations IS WHAT WE DO as human begins. When creating a strategy for oneself, or in business, or education, or for government, it is important to remember this fact. Humans begin every journey—in essence cannot stop themselves from—gathering information and looking for patterns. It's how we relate to the world and to one another. Asking questions and then taking action to respond to what we've perceived is our job. It's our nature.

Now, so that we do not violate a basic principle and make things too complicated, let's simply say, that these things may be beyond our scope at this time. They are certainly beyond what we are trying to accomplish in this book. Acknowledge the dilemma and the beauty of the paradox and move forward. The symbol of the circle is used to represent life, because it is without beginning or end. The triangle, another symbol for Ultimate Truth is often referenced to depict the relationship between of Mind, Body and Spirit. Both symbols are empty at the center but flow between concepts. Life is defined by death and death is the ultimate paradox. We can never really know the answer to the question that drives our entire lives. Yet, we cannot stop obsessing about the question.

"To be or not to be, that is the question..."

—Hamlet, from Shakespeare's Hamlet, Prince Of Denmark

Chapter Three

THE PRINCIPLE OF FORM

Simply put, the second Principle of Everything states: ***Everything that we can become aware of has a form (method, way, applicable rules, etc.) and the form is best considered within the context of the five principles.*** In other words, while applying our tendency to look for patterns, there appears to be a certain order that is favored by the Universe itself. These patterns are sometimes obvious to us and become commonplace and useful in our everyday lives. When that happens we say that our patterns are routine. On the other hand, when we obsess over the form, rather than the goal that the form was trying to achieve, we call that ritual. Looking for patterns and/or meaning in our lives is one of the major attributes of being human. If it weren't for this tendency to find patterns, then most scientific discoveries would never have been made. It is how language is developed. In terms of The Five Principles we often say, "There are a lot of different ways to accomplish the same thing." This is especially cogent if (as we've previously implied) Awareness of the Five Principles is the ultimate goal in itself.

Speaking of science, in the martial science of ninjitsu we refer to the "geometry" of the universe by way of describing useful and realistic body movements. The "way" that a "good" punch or kick is thrown, is based upon the firsthand experiences of the "grandmasters" who have developed their styles on the awareness of "what works." I've also heard geometric terms used in fine arts classes or for humanities or sciences. In all cases this geometry focus tells us that there are only two geometric forms in the observable universe: straight lines and curves (curves result in circles). In martial arts we see that there is a tendency to move our hands and feet either in straight lines or in circular motions. In drawing we see that all shapes are made of these two types of lines.

Sometimes we uncover information about universal or macro physical patterns through our knowledge and observation of these smaller patterns. A good case in point is made by how black holes were discovered mathematically, for instance. Today scientists accept the existence of black holes that were only once inferred by mathematical equations. Our human rules and methods are usually an attempt to imitate "or become aware" of what we perceive to be the "order of the universe" and the "universal laws" that govern it. In martial arts we acknowledge a direct connection between what we do and "why" we do it. In tai chi, for instance we say that proper form promotes an awareness of chi, or truth, or oneness or nirvana or God or the theory/equation that answers all questions. We may have other objectives in mind, but there's always a right way of doing everything. Some belief systems have gone so far as to say that without the form, or the way or the ritual, that an awareness of the all (the ultimate awareness) would be unattainable. In other words, for some *form is everything.*

Again, we do not have to always know why this is so, but there should be a reliable, simple way of testing whether something is done correctly. This relates to the way things are as well the way they are meant to be.

In martial arts we ask, "*What works best?*" One of the five basic parts of a self-defense technique is "defend yourself." If a technique does not accomplish this goal, then it is no good, no matter how spectacular it looks. The "gold standard" in martial arts has often been considered to be the Shaolin/five animal styles that are taught by the monks at the Shaolin Temple in China. As with many cultures, the original creators of these "styles" of martial arts, observed nature, and animals looking for patterns and "strengths" in style and function that were worthy of being imitated. This is how the "five animal" system of kung fu was created. These animals eventually became associated with the "five powers" that the Chinese believed governed the universe.

Many cultures look to nature to find patterns (strengths) that coincide with Ultimate Powers that appear to govern the operation of all things. When you build anything of value, you must proceed from a plan. We need a good foundation from which to build every house. A Successful Life Strategy is a kind of plan of action that works. However, instead of embroiling ourselves in endless debates about which plan is right or why one plan is better than another, a Five Principle approach looks to find the common ground for all plans. On the other hand, just because someone has a plan, doesn't mean that there is any truth to it. Where would such a plan diverge from the truth? A false plan (or ineffective one) is one that violates the simple, basic principles of our universe, or of our individual right to pursue awareness. If one person group or individual believes that they have the right to harm another group or individual because of their "rightness" then we could see that the plan is flawed.

Form, ritual and repetition are plans, in a sense, that deal with learning on various levels, and any ritual or repeated action or thought will get results. This is one reason that cults exist and sometimes flourish. People "feel a difference" when they act or think in a prescribed way. This is why, however we emphasize that there is "no one correct way" and that an obsession with one of the principles (such as the principle of benefit) as being the "ultimate goal" indicates a strategy that is fatally flawed.

With a Five Principles Strategy, we say there are right stances, right positions, right ways of breathing, right times, right sounds, right tensions, right order, right atmosphere and even right ways of thinking or feeling. All of this implies that there are also wrong ways of doing the same things. The difference between the two may only be one of emphasis.

The Principle of Form suggests that right form, first of all, should be easy to determine from wrong form. Secondly (and possibly more importantly) right form can be determined from wrong by the simple test that it must never violate any of the other basic principles. Right form also has obvious benefits and sticks to the "point" as well as the ultimate objectives.

When we accept that there is a reason for action and that there is a proper course to take, then we must have the courage to act accordingly. Action, for human beings, is often equated with courage. As with everything, however, the counterpart (inaction) must also be an option and be applied, at times, as part of a Successful Life Strategy. Running away or going out of ones way to avoid conflict will always achieve the desired goal, if failure (defeat) is out of the question. Without violating the other basic principles of chi, then, The Five Principle exercises stress that there is a time to move and a time to be still. There is a time to be tense and a time to be relaxed. The length of time we must relax, or be tense, also varies according to the situation and other conditions. There is even a correct framework for our thought processes.

When I teach writing classes, I emphasize that "communication" is the key objective of ALL forms of interaction (speaking, reading, writing, performance etc.). There are "ways" or forms that seem to allow communication to occur "best." We like to feel that there is "order" in the perceivable world, but we have come to expect it in our communication skills. For these reasons, I also tell my students that their "words have power" and that a sentence, a paragraph, an essay, a poem, a script, an email, a text message, even a shopping note that we leave to ourselves on the refrigerator door all have certain things in common. The first and most important thing is that "we are trying to communicate" and a simple test for "right" and "wrong" form is simply: "Did we accomplish this simple objective?"

We also see there are other similarities of form. Each "form" of communication has a "proper" beginning, middle and end. In many cultures there is a sense that The Spirit or God or Universal Mind has a recognizable form. Some go so far as to say that we are "created in the image of God." I think that this is intuitively, absolutely true. However, that does not mean that the Spiritual Mind or The Universe is created in humanity's image. We should take this statement's truth to be based upon the same five principles that appear to be at work in our own physical, mental and spiritual lives. So, as Five Principlists we say, "It appears that the Universe and our own physical essence have similar "forms." From that, we deduce that perhaps this "sameness" can be witnessed, not in our human form, but in the form that "life" and "awareness" seem to take. Perhaps, then the Great Spirit, or Creator resembles more a strand of DNA than a human being. In the end, all these explanations are mere speculation (unknowable) until such time as we are moved, by circumstance, technology or other advancement to catch a glimpse of the Spirit itself, and measure this likeness against some other known pattern.

Some cultures (and here we include many philosophers and scientists) believe that everything is made up of the same essential stuff and then they go about trying to prove the ultimate answer for everything.

Native Americans, Africans, Australian Aborigines, Europeans, Polynesians and Asian cultures all believe that we not only are "made of the same stuff as God" but that we can "imitate or make contact with the Spirit and represent the Spiritual Laws" in a variety of artistic ways (forms). The Hindus have divided these "forms" along the lines of our senses and under the sub-headings of Mudra, Midra or Mandela. With these divisions we end up in other cultures, Navaho, Tibetan for instance with similar forms which utilize an awareness of audio, visual and textual representations of universal laws and beliefs.

In Five Birds Martial Arts, the martial arts concepts and the tai chi like stances and positions are like becoming your own acupuncture needles or becoming part of your own sand painting, where you get to play the part of the finished product, as well as each individual grain of sand. You are PART of the form and the instrument by which success or "enlightenment" is measured.

To be certain that form does not become an obsession, violating any of the other basic principles, we suggest performing any exercises (including those suggested at the end of this book) with effort being devoted to flowing from one position to the next, with an equal effort given to the individual steps in the forms themselves. In writing, one may study structure or grammar, or the relationship between speaking, reading and writing for example, but should never lose sight of the ultimate goal for all three of these skills…communication.

From a Life Strategy or Five Principle perspective, we say that the right form is one that takes into account both the individual and the universal objectives. Our scale is sometimes called, "Total Fitness." A valid Total Fitness strategy should take into account more than one end of the spectrum. In fact, in this perspective the method we often use to teach one thing is by describing its opposite.

However, we are not really concerned with the individual opposites, but rather the Ultimate Subtle Essence, which exists between the opposites, because and in spite of them. Similarities are ultimately more important than differences, if for no other reason than that is how we are made.

"Howsoever men try to worship Me, so do I welcome them. By whatever path they travel, it leads to Me, at last."
— The Supreme Spirit, from, Bhagavad-Gita

"Politics are divine sciences after all. The science of government it is my duty to study... I must study politics and war, that our sons may have liberty to study mathematics and philosophy. Our sons ought to study mathematics and philosophy, geography, natural history... commerce and agriculture in order to give their children a right to study painting, poetry, music, architecture, statuary, tapestry and porcelain."—John Adams

Chapter Four

THE PRINCIPLE OF BENEFIT

In martial arts we often talk about how effective a technique is or is not. There are, I've said, five parts of every successful self-defense technique (the only thing of importance to note is that there are five parts). Within the context of all "technique" the first and foremost question that all martial artists ask themselves is this: "Does the technique (form) work? Does it accomplish its goal? Does it help you to defend yourself?" This again may seem too obvious. However, in many styles of martial arts, the student is so engrossed in trying to follow the "way of the master," and copying the master's movements that they simply become dysfunctional. At that point, the adherence to what is perceived as the "strength" of a style becomes its weakness, because of the lack of attention to the principle of benefit. An obsession with only the Principle of Awareness, Form, Flow, Harmony or Benefit will ultimately lead to failure, because this obsession is outside the natural order. No one part of the whole can ever be more important than the sum total. Yet, from an individual's perspective there must also be a payoff, without disrupting the flow for the common good.

In business, we hear phrases like, "whether it is the sale of goods or services, the customer must feel they are getting good value for their investment."

We see that an obsession with benefit leads only to failure again and again in life. When politicians try to make common laws that benefit only a small minority or are true only to one narrow ideology or to one segment of society, then conflicts develop. By the same token, since the universe appears to favor order, if an ideology creates conflicts then the ideology or system should be suspect. We should not pretend that any of the opposing parties within the conflict are the problem that needs to be solved. It is this narrow thinking that seeks to demonize opposing opinions within a debate, rather than focusing on the actual question at hand.

If we miss a shot in tennis, we should not fault the net, court, our opponent, or the game of tennis itself. We also should not strive to alter the game of tennis to fit our mistakes. Perhaps tennis is simply not our sport.

If we strike out at the plate in baseball, we should not try to make the pitcher throw more slowly over a smaller plate or force him to carry a sack of sand on his back, just to make it more fair.

When I teach English composition, I suggest that students see writing a sentence, a paragraph and a finished composition in any form (essay, story, poem, script etc.) as the "form" of the strategy that they want to succeed with. The benefit, in all cases is communication. Big words, jumbled on a page, without punctuation or capitalization are nonsense. Words, in a format that is understandable, has a clear focus, a beginning, middle and end and an obvious point of view will demonstrate the power of words and are more likely to communicate whatever it was the writer felt was important to say.

So, we proceed along this line of thinking and are likely to conclude, "If any one of the principles is violated by following the other four, then the overall system is in need of adjustment." In other words, it does not appear that the Universe "picks and chooses" how and when it follows the laws that guide it. So, why should we?" Therefore, if a strategy, a technique, a plan or even a simple action loses sight of these basic principles (or loses sight of the goal it was initially set up to try and accomplish) then it should not be pursued.

The Principle of Benefit assumes that The Universe functions in an orderly manner. Mathematical calculations can be applied to everything. So, to put it simply, we conclude that, *"The Universe tries to benefit itself, or that while our actions have results (and sometimes we don't really understand the full extent of that statement) there seems to be a tendency to reward action that is in common good."*

In the understanding and application of this Principle of Benefit, we would not be overstating the importance by saying, that benefit is everything.

I really don't like to even use the word "exercises" for anything that I teach, because this implies to many that energy is EXPENDED in an effort to learn. I say that one of the basic principles of martial arts is that whatever you do to become aware of these universal principles should "make you feel better."

There is the old joke that illustrates this point. A man walks into a doctor's office and says, "Doc, it hurts when I move my leg like this." The doctor responds, "Well, don't do that."

Some people believe that humans can increase their personal powers and that they can use these powers for good or evil. If we look logically at the Principles of Everything, we can see that this is simply cannot be the case. Humans can, indeed do harm to one another or to themselves. However, the designation of "good" or "evil" is a human one. While a concept may be motivational, or even essential to a belief system it's important to remember that we are human.

Recently (at the time of this writing) a famous terrorist was killed by elite U.S. SEAL forces. As he was ultimately responsible for the Twin Towers tragedy that occurred on 9/11 in New York, I do not want to give his memory any impetus by naming him here. Let it suffice to say that "most" people saw the action as just. Some, who wanted to find justification for their belief that "killing is wrong," asked the Dalai Lama what his position was on the assassination. He said, in essence, "I believe that life is sacred. I do not like to take any life, even that of a mosquito. However, when I am in a malaria prone country, I will kill these insects if they land on my skin."

Universal Energy flows, essentially only for its own good. Our tiny actions, thoughts and constructs are microcosms of the greater, universal principles. Therefore, evil acts or even thoughts of human beings are generally considered to be only an interruption in the natural order of things at the human level.

Illness, for instance in most Eastern thought, is understood to be merely an interruption of the flow of universal chi, or energy. This is not a new concept, or just an Eastern one. Being a good (or healthy) human is generally considered to be one that pursues individual goals (happiness) as part of the natural order of things. In other words, seeking a benefit of our actions—a natural and true goal—is a measure of the value of the action, as long as that action does not interfere with anyone else's pursuit of happiness.

Within this we must add that individual pleasure is not true happiness, nor ultimately a benefit that one should base a life-strategy on pursing. This is like believing that getting a passing grade on a quiz is more important that learning the subject.

Pleasure is short lived, and only a hoped for byproduct of the bigger picture inherent in benefit. The pursuit of happiness (if seen as the ultimate benefit) has long term and wide-reaching affects. Pleasure deals mainly with the physical senses, while happiness (often giving us the sense of physical sensation) is really experienced on a much deeper level. To think that pleasure IS happiness, is as wrong as believing that the blue print IS the house, or that visiting or reading about a place is the same as living there.

What we stress in The Five Principles approach is that our ultimate goals are natural or universal ones. Satisfaction, health, wellbeing, and connectedness (learning and communication) are really all found at a level that is a unification of the individual principles. In martial arts and many other philosophies, the triangle or trinity is an all-important symbol. When we talk of Benefit, we believe that adherence to the Five Basic Principles will benefit us at the levels of Mind, Body and Spirit ...as well as the undefined place in between.

The Constitution of the United States of America is a powerful document because, I believe, the main author (Thomas Jefferson) tried to adhere to these basic universal principles. The ultimate purposes of the document are coincidentally five. These goals and benefits are summed up in words of the preamble, “We the People of the United States, in Order to form a more perfect Union, establish Justice, insure domestic Tranquility, provide for the common defense, promote the general Welfare, and secure the Blessings of Liberty to ourselves and our Posterity, do ordain and establish this Constitution for the United States of America.”

These five purposes echo those found in the Declaration of Independence in the simple yet enduring phrase, “Life, Liberty and the Pursuit of Happiness.” Until that time, those goals (especially liberty) had never been considered as “inalienable rights” or primary ones for establishing a government. However, never forget that “Common

Tranquility, Defense and General Welfare" are how this awareness (definition of liberty) is being qualified and defined. Awareness is being focused, through the physical structure of a government document, to move a people forward into the future of a common good.

The principle of benefit can be summed up in the statement, "If we are not getting something out of the activity we are performing, at a spiritual, mental and physical level, then we probably shouldn't be doing it."

The Universal Subtle Essence is unnamable and omnipresent.

Although it appears even in the plainest and most ordinary of things, it is inferior to nothing.

It maintains itself as a model of indivisible integrity.

If people would embrace it as their own true nature, everything would settle down in right order and peace of its own accord.

Harmonious relationship can be illustrated by the cycle of the seasons which produces rain and dew at exactly the right times.

People do not need to do anything to insure harmony between Heaven And Earth.

All names were given for the purpose of distinction when the original simplicity was diversified.

When one departs from simplicity, the result is perplexity. When one returns to simplicity, one is saved from destruction by confusion. The Universal Subtle Essence is to human beings, what the great ocean is to the rivers and streams of the Earth.

—Lao Tzu, from *Tao Teh Ching*

Chapter Five

THE PRINCIPLE OF HARMONY

The final Principle of Everything is Harmony, also known as Balance, Relativity or Adaptability. Again, because we strive for both brevity and clarity, we must proceed from certain assumptions:

1) Human beings are born to be creative and 2) Change is inevitable. If we are not allowed to look over the next horizon, reevaluate information and then reinvent the wheel, we generally end up feeling stifled. Allowing oneself a certain amount of wiggle-room to change or create new options. In fact, this appears to be a requirement for happiness (or fulfillment, or inevitability). You insert the term you prefer.

Life is full of subtle yet profound changes...a process from youth through aging, from innocence to wisdom all within the same body that never seems to stay the same. Not accepting our inbred "operating system" has been the downfall of many a personal relationship, especially when one individual sets stagnation or non-change as a condition for success. Another way of summarizing this principle is to say, "Perspective is everything."

In martial arts, we talk about another part of every self-defense technique being "lowering your center of gravity." A person's balance, in relationship to his opponent's is a crucial factor in success. Another side of this same coin is called "a willingness to abandon technique."

This concept was called, *Letting Go Of The Hilt* by the swordsman, Musashi. Here he is suggesting that if a sword-fighting technique is learned and practiced, but is not working, we must have the sense to give it up, or alter it, so that it can accomplish its purpose. Musashi was known as the greatest swordsman in feudal Japan, but he suggested that there might be times when (even a great swordsman) must let go of the sword to accomplish your true goal. In his case, the goal was simple: defeating the enemy. There is one great tale of how this swordsman fought and defeated an attacker with a wet oar and his bare fists. He always kept sight of his true goal and did not allow his preconceptions to limit his options.

In the fighting style that I favor, we call this tendency to "stick to an ideology or a technique or any other specific methodology" as being "weapon stupid," and therefore something to be avoided.

Naturally, it is valuable to have a moment to reflect and decide on our strategy (sometimes represented by the void).

However, the more options we have, the more actions we can take comfortably in any given situation, the better off we will be (adaptability). Having the freedom of skilled choice is true freedom.

One of the greatest lessons I received from a Lakota Pipe Carrier (medicine person) was to "whenever possible, think before responding to any question of worth." I noticed that sometimes, when I asked a direct question, these teachers would simply walk away as if they hadn't heard me. At first, I thought I had asked an inappropriate (dare I say stupid) question and my teachers did not feel it was worthy of a response. This assumption could not have been farther from the truth, as it turns out. Once, after seemingly being ignored I realized that as suddenly as my teachers had departed, out of the blue at a later time, they reappeared and were giving me an answer to a question that I might have already forgotten. When I saw what was happening, I asked about the process and was told that many "people of power" feel as though they have an obligation to give the best advice they can, especially when asked for it. If an answer to a question was not obvious to the teacher (especially the Lakota apparently) they felt they could take *up to three days* to respond. My teacher told me that it was kind of an "unwritten rule," because of his rank in the tribe, that he was allowed extra time to "become comfortable" with the question before responding. In other words, by his definition he had to be in harmony or balance between the response and the query.

It must be stated here that perspective is also ever changing and that our very concept of what constitutes a Universe today is an ever-changing one. Today, scientists (not just those considered wild-eyed mystics) are talking about Multi-verses and within that there are many different theories and conjectures about how these new, quantum physics version of reality might be viewed.

This complicates things for those who are looking to unify all theories (or those who believe there is ONE right way of doing everything). Although physicists are constantly in search of this unifying theory (a theory of everything) to explain and justify all the other theories, the "bulls eye" on the target not only continues to move, but might actually disappear from a single, narrow interpretation of reality.

A Japanese Zen Master who was teaching me about Kyudo (Zen Archery) described the situation like this: "People come to me and ask me to teach them archery. They see learning to meditate in this way as a goal, like climbing to the top of a particular mountain. The mountain that I sit on top of is not necessarily the highest mountain or the best mountain, but they see me as sitting on top of a mountain that they want to climb. Every student comes to me from different directions and they don't see that from where I sit, I have a good view of all the directions. I see the obstacles that they have to overcome to reach where I am. I can see, for instance that one student has a clear path to the top of the mountain, so I tell them to go straight ahead. Another student may have his or her way blocked by a river or a forest, so I guide them accordingly. The problem is that sometimes one student hears me give directions to another to go straight ahead, while I tell them to turn left or right and the first thinks they are being treated unfairly. They ignore my directions and start to follow the directions I'm giving to the other students. They can never benefit from my instruction because they end up lost in the forest or falling into the river. A good teacher however must be true to his position and continue to answer the question of 'how do I get to the top of your mountain?' honestly and responsibly. Hopefully, most students will realize the teacher's intent is pure and will eventually make it to their goal."

There are many martial arts styles that rely only on ONE PART OF A STRATEGY, which is an easy thing to do if success has been achieved in the past. However, just because one individual, with a particular skill and bent of nature succeeded with a specific technique, under specific conditions...it doesn't mean that this technique or “style” will work for everyone under every circumstance. On the other hand, we can't deny success. That is why, I believe, we have such devotion to the words of the masters (you can inject the term highly successful individuals here, if it makes you more comfortable). People have certainly achieved success, for themselves, in a variety of ways. That doesn't mean that they can (or should) teach other's that the way they have succeeded is the ONLY way to achieve success. By mastering any one concept (principle of chi or part of a successful life strategy) some can indeed see a certain level of success. Hence the saying, "If it isn't broke, don't fix it."

However, when it comes to true happiness, true freedom or true awareness we can say, for the Ultimate Success, an attention to Harmony is everything. In many cultures, the place where all the other strategies or powers come together is known as the void, or emptiness. To achieve emptiness or nothingness is believed to be the ultimate goal.

Problems exist with this line of thinking. One problem with understanding Void comes in the relative size and relationship to the thing we are discussing. In other words, emptiness can be either so small or so vast, that it is beyond our perceptions. Knowing that emptiness exists may be all we can expect in any given situation. In fact, accepting the existence of nothingness might well be an essential step to achieving true happiness!

For instance, there is a famous philosophical proposition about a fly crashing headlong into a locomotive that is racing straight toward it on a railroad track. To tempt our logic, the question is posed: Is there a point at which the fly changes direction from straightforward to straight backward? Does this mean that the fly (and therefore the locomotive) must both stop completely?

The principle of Harmony says that there is a proper time for moving forward and for moving backward and for not moving at all. We should be aware of the extremes, their opposites and the point at which we change from one direction to the other. We should also know our limitations. Some people (mathematicians and philosophers for the most part) have actually told me that it can be proven that the locomotive indeed stops for an instant. Others have argued passionately against the idea. Does it matter to my everyday life? For me this kind of thinking remains interesting on the level that it highlights our basic need to pose queries and create hypotheses. Information gathering and speculation about everything will never be a worthless pursuit. Whether we like it or not, human beings are lifelong learners.

If we are completely unable to benefit from an idea or action though, then we should abandon it for the moment and try something else. I return to the Constitution of the United States of America for a moment and point out that "adaptability" is an essential quality that makes this document work. From the very beginning our founding fathers knew that there needed to be mechanisms in place to change our laws, as situations change. Indeed, they changed this document almost immediately by adding the Bill of Rights, and amendments have been added and repealed ever since.

Movement and stillness, tension and relaxation, thinking and feeling all have appropriate times and places. Human beings, exercising a proper responsibility to all the forces that surround them, learn to balance their lives with these contradictory forces, so that they can receive the benefits of all.

The definition of "beneficial" is also always subject to the peculiarities of the time, place and situation (as we've seen in a previous chapter). Again, we never know when a piece of information is going to be of use to us. Likewise, we never know how our actions or words are going to affect others. I often tell the following story to my students: Before I worked as a teacher in L.A. County Jails, I worked with emotionally disturbed children at a facility called Hathaway.

During my close to seven years there, I worked with hundreds of kids and learned a lot from each of them. During this time, I was working on obtaining my Master of Arts degree and on my first black belt. Part of the job was that we lived in a house with about twenty kids for two and a half days each week. Staff was rotated so that there were always two "house parents" on duty at all times. While living in the house for my shift, I had to practice martial arts while the children were asleep. One boy, about ten years of age, sneaked out to watch me while I practiced and we formed a strong bond. The reason I let him hedge on his bedtime and his unusual attachment to me was that he was a half white/half Indian kid who had formed a strong bond to a character in the movie, BILLY JACK. This character was also half-white and half-Indian, a Viet Nam War vet who had returned to the reservation to save an Indian School from local evils. The local evil took the form of unscrupulous white ranchers who were illegally hunting and capturing wild horses for the dog food trade and who also hated anything related to Native Americans or hippies. Billy Jack's tools for keeping the kids safe were his hands and feet and "Green Beret tricks" he'd learned while serving in Viet Nam. Oh, I forgot to mention that Billy Jack had a signature black, round-topped, flat brimmed hat. The boy who wanted to watch me at night-we'll call him Little Billy—also wore one of these hats. Little Billy had been badly abused by adults growing up, I was told, and when I made the connection between Little Billy's heritage and his association with the Billy Jack character, I realized that it made him feel safer to know that someone was practicing martial arts in the same house where he slept, just as wearing the Billy Jack hat made him feel less vulnerable. I also encouraged Little Billy to be proud of his Native heritage and told him about some of my teachers and of the great heroes of the American past who were his ancient relatives. We shared some good moments together and eventually he was removed from the therapeutic environment of the Village.

Now, we need to flash-forward about 20 years. I was teaching ESL, GED preparation, drug and alcohol abuse prevention and high school diploma subjects within the L.A. County Jails to the inmates, sitting in my classroom with about 50 inmate-students when the phone rang. This was a little unusual, in itself, since I got very few calls in jail. However, what was stranger was when I picked up the receiver and a voice at the other end said, "Hello sir. I'm looking for Gordon Richiusa, sir." Immediately there was recognition.

"Little Billy? Is that you?"

"Yes, sir. I didn't think you'd remember me sir."

"Billy," I said, interrupting. "Have you been in the service?"

"Yes, Sir," he responded. "How did you know, sir?"

"Billy, you can stop calling me Sir," I said, and then quickly added. "I can't believe this. How did you get through on this line? How did you find me? Why are you calling?"

Billy told me that he had left the home where I worked with him, had gotten his high school diploma and his black belt and then joined the service. He had served honorably and was discharged after which he had pursued him heritage and found his maternal grandfather on the Piute Reservation in Nevada. His grandfather was a medicine man in the tribe and had agreed to teach Billy the old ways.

"Congratulations," I told him. "But, why are you calling me now?"

"I was in a ceremony recently and I had a vision of you telling me the one thing that had changed my life for the better. I just wanted to let you know and to thank you."

For some reason I was stunned. Billy told me that he had been hunting for me for a couple of weeks, going back to Hathaway then following leads until finally finding out that I was working in jail. He then had to get the education department's phone number and convince a few receptionists to put him through to the phone I was talking on, all because I had finally said something memorable that had benefited someone's life in a profound way. I couldn't wait to hear what these words were that had affected him so much that he felt he had to find me.

"So what did I say?"

"You told me that there are two ways to breathe."

I admit that I was a little deflated. This did not seem profound at any level and I did not immediately remember the context in which I had imparted this questionable wisdom. "Could you please explain?" I asked.

Billy went on to remind me that often the children in our care would have what we lovingly referred to as, "freak outs." These were emotional displays, tantrums of monumental proportions in some cases. Billy was legendary in his writhing, howling and frothing exhibitions, so much so that during one episode four grown adults where holding him down in a panic shouting directions such as "Calm down! CALM DOWN!"

When I saw what was happening, I lay down on the floor next to Billy's head, with my face next to his and said, "I know this is going to be hard Billy, but these staff members are not going to let you go until you calm down. When you calm down, they will calm down. I want you to try something. Just notice the way you are breathing." He was near hyperventilating, rapidly panting between growls. Try thinking about nothing else except your breathing. If you can slow your breathing, you will relax. When you relax, they will let you go."

Billy said that not only did it work in this situation, but also it was probably the most significant piece of information in his later successes. You never know what affect your words or actions are going to have on others. The best we can do is to deal with every situation honestly, honorably and with respect that each action may be of far greater significance that we realize in the heat of the moment. As a person who calls himself a teacher, it's a big responsibility that I take more seriously now. I thanked Billy for calling me and got his permission to tell this story to others.

The conditions of a Solitary Bird are five.
The first is that he flies to the highest point.
The second is that he points his beak to the sky.
The third is that he does not suffer for want of company, not even of his own kind.
The fourth is that he has no definite color.
And, the fifth is that he sings very softly.
—*San Juan De la Cruz,* The Conditions Of a Solitary Bird

"A plain glass of water can become the most powerful medicine, if given in the proper spirit."
Lame Deer Erdoes, From Lame Deer, Seeker of Vision.

Chapter Six

AFTERWORD

There once was a teacher who made a very succinct illustration, illuminating the difference between Achieving the Ultimate Benefit of Meditation and not achieving it. He said, "We can get up and walk across the room OR (changing the tone of his voice) we can rise and walk across the room." Explaining further he said, "In other words, we can move randomly and uncoordinated OR with focus and control, fully aware, in harmony with the forces of nature, without violating any morals or ethics, we can make the choice to rise and then act with full responsibility by walking across the room, head held high, fully aware of our actions, as if they are a matter of life and death."

This way of looking at things turns every act (or inaction) into an act of power. By applying the Five Principles of Chi to our thoughts, words and deeds, we can transform our lives from their current levels to the miraculous. By practicing Go-Tao-Chi, in whatever way possible, we allow our bodies and our minds to flow, to assist each other in a coordinated effort for true happiness.

I've been studying and practicing martial arts of all types for almost fifty years. That does NOT, by any means, make me a MASTER (since I don't believe such a state exists). However, I do believe that my experience and dedication to the study of all forms of martial arts has allowed me a unique advantage from which to make certain observations about the similarities and differences in the styles I've studied. In speculating about how my training has benefited and affected me, I've been forced to find new and better ways to explain what I do. In the process, I have arrived at what I feel are the best ways to pass on what I've learned to others. In most cases, those who have dedicated their lives to the profession of teaching have handed the lessons I've learned to me. It doesn't matter what the source discipline is or if the teachers considered themselves professionals. A good teacher is one who has something of worth to impart and has figured out a way (or ways, which also usually includes being a good example) to communicate this information, fact, style, technique, perspective, idea or value.

So, in the end, during the course of my training (and again, I want to thank all of those who have taken the time to teach me), I've become a teacher. From this perspective, I've developed and now teach a system of teaching, rather than a specific style of martial arts. I call the overall blueprint for learning The Five Bird System, and strive to achieve and teach a disciplined approach to Total Fitness.

I have also come to the conclusion that concepts are much more important in a well rounded training program, then any particular technique, art or piece of equipment.

Here are some of the concepts that I work with:

1) A martial artist's discipline offers a great advantage to the success of Total Fitness.

2) The Brain is the best weapon.

3) Faith and trust in our feelings are our best prevention of having to defend ourselves.

I use the Okinawan form of karate known as Goju Ryu as the foundation for the empty hand training, which is the heart of the overall teaching. I have chosen this "style" as a foundation because I know it best, and because the name means "Hard-Soft Way." However, I supplement what I teach, with any form of healthful movement that a student should like to participate in. I believe in the adage: the best form of exercise is the one that an individual will do on a regular basis. Along these lines, I require that each student who wishes to attain Advanced Instructor or Black Belt status with me, also bring something into the art, by applying what they've learned through demonstration of a SPECIAL SKILL. In times gone by it was common for the best students to "earn" their lessons with actions such as cooking or cleaning or other manual labor in exchange for training. I add to this knowledge my own, free form training, a number of other martial arts that I've had the good fortune to study over the years, and a bit of personal observation.

I have become a professional teacher because of my attention to my students as well as to my own peculiar way of learning. I feel that learning to teach is my own personal expression of the highest form of achievement for my awareness. In fact, the student teacher relationship, in itself, is merely a model of the natural condition of parent-child, which is another great way to exhibit the Five Principles Approach.

As a teacher, if I hear or see something that makes sense to me, then I quote liberally. The result of what I now do with a student, I call Concept Training, because it emphasizes the underlying concepts, rather than specific techniques. In the past two decades I've trained, literally hundreds if not thousands of students in what I have been taught about martial arts. I also acknowledge a great number of others as my teachers.

I hope I never stop learning. Some of the lessons that I have absorbed are that times are changing. The needs of people are different then they used to be and, most importantly, how people learn is also, always in flux. What may be good for one time period, geographic location or culture, may not suit another. In fact, there was always a personal flaw to every art that I had studied. That means that there was always something that did not feel quite right to me, or strike me as true. It was in this atmosphere that I developed Five Birds Martial Arts and the Five Principles of Everything. I realize, as I write this, that there are those who will just not get it or will say (rightfully) that this book does not meet their needs. There will also be those who will take exception with my comparison of Tai Chi or other martial arts to Go-Tao-Chi or the Five Principles. To them, I apologize. I know that tai chi (you may insert any other discipline here that will make you feel good) is absolutely perfect for some.

I am not trying to denigrate any art, pursuit, skill, business, religion or discipline. Obviously, with the attention that I give to tai-chi forms, I also have benefited from the study of this art. I also have tried yoga and weightlifting. I just didn't learn any of these forms as the *only* ones worth pursuing. For that I am grateful to the wisdom of my own teachers.

In the end, all I am really trying to do with The Five Principles is narrow the concepts down to the most essential units for my own benefit.

By so doing, I learn how to apply these concepts to actions or techniques, which I know to be beneficial (since I've benefited from them). In the end, I will always only be able to state what I believe and allow a seeker of knowledge, a student of martial arts or any endeavor, to follow or reject the Concept of Total Fitness. They can see for themselves if The Five Principles of Everything help them in their pursuits. Or, they can totally reject them.

For my part, I must believe this book helps you in some way. I believe that when a person adheres to the Five Principles of Everything, the results will be a sense of accomplishment, a well-rounded exercise program, an increase in Defense Awareness or a Second attention, a development of a Successful Life Strategy, a feeling of balance and well-being and a general increase in physical health. In all cases, success will be measured in very specific and personal terms...as it must be, and the best teaching strategy is that which Randy Pausch formulated in his last lecture: *Don't try to teach. Just tell stories.*

So here's a final story: Let's say, for the sake of argument that human beings are like a sailboat on a large body of water, moving with the wind. The boat is not the wind, nor is it the water or the trees from which the lumber that built the boat was cut. However, to achieve its Ultimate Goal of Self Actualization, the boat must be put together according to a proper plan, and use the wind and the water to its best advantage. The boat, in a sense, must be totally self-aware and Open At All Eight Corners. The wind and the water have many similarities, but they are not the same thing. When the boat interacts with either, we might say that it is like the wind, or at the mercy of the water. Neither one of these statements is ultimately true.

The more that the sailor in the boat knows about the subjects of wind or water, or even the boat itself, will aid him or her in guiding the vessel to the ultimate destination...where ever that happens to be. Sometimes the water is smooth, or rough, or has strong currents, and the weight inside the boat must be shifted or the tiller (steering mechanism) must be turned slightly to compensate. The sailor and the boat, benefit from knowledge, observation of the water and intuition. If the water is warm or shallow, the boat will sail a certain way. If the water freezes or is deep, other conditions exist that must be dealt with.

With the wind, the unseen, it is the same. The focus and control of the boat to its destination can only hope for a favorable wind, then trim the sail properly to the wind that is made available.

Five Principles perspective makes available power, the relationship and result of the interaction of boat, wind and water, without dwelling on any one of them.

Chapter Seven

Abstracts & Additional Illustrative Articles

The following sections show how to use the Five Principles in various, specific forms. The first is an introduction to the Illustrative Articles, followed by an explanation of The Five Bird System that appears in Volume Four, Martial Arts Entertainment Magazine and on WorldWideDojo.com.

Forward to Abstracts

By Ed Tao

When I first met Gordon Richiusa, it was in the spring of 2009 when I enrolled in the non-fiction writing class from Saddleback College Emeritus Institute that he was teaching. I was very impressed with how Gordon stimulates students' inner desire and abilities to engage in very profound thinking and discussions. What was of particular interest to me is his lifetime passion for marital arts. Since this is my own personal interest going back to my post high school days, I found a special affinity with Gordon. Toward the end of the semester, Gordon gave me a copy of his book, Go-Tao-Chi, The Five Principles of Chi.

Later on, we had numerous discussions about the book and various subjects relating to martial arts. I was very impressed by Gordon's knowledge of many things in addition to his commonly known specialties. For me, the beauty of this approach is its simplicity and wide applicability to so many areas. Using his systems and based upon his decades of writing, Gordon has been awarded a Lifetime Achievement Award and inducted into two martial arts Halls of Fame. He is also an accomplished writer, teacher and profound thinker with a broad and varied academic and professional background. The more I learned about Gordon, the more I realized how he had developed all his special skills from the same simple perspective of the five principles. He even taught the subject of Writing in English using the same terms. All the while, he never asked me to abandon my own paths, or change my perspective, but merely led by example.

Eventually, I started to apply the "Go-Tao-Chi" principles—the name he was calling the five principles by in those days—to my own writing, tai chi practice, other sports activities (i.e., tennis, golfing) and personal interests (super healthy communities and health related practices). To my pleasant surprise, applying these principles always works very well. When I reviewed the reasons why, I realized that the Five Principles perspective has some of the same ingredients as commonly taught by masters and great teachers from many varied disciplines in the past. I consider myself a good student, and since I am accustomed to tai chi practice (which I started since 1972), let me use tai chi as an example to demonstrate the Five Principles as related to my own experience.

In tai chi practice, it is very important to realize the nature and reasoning behind the lessons.

The two principles Awareness - Principle#1 and its Benefit-Principle#4 are very much related, and like any human activity, need to be updated to suit the ever changing circumstances of how and why this form is practiced (Form-Principle # 2 and 5 Harmony-Principle #5). For example, in early days, when tai chi practice was at its peak; it was as premier defensive martial arts with health benefits as a secondary objective. In today's environment, the health benefits are often used as primary reasons for people to study tai chi and other related skills. Since the emergence of Chinese "Qigong" started in China in the late '70's; the "awareness" of various styles of Chinese Qigong, with some of its amazing health "benefits" needs to be re-incorporated to update the modern tai chi practice.

Started in 1992, I have had the opportunity to study Chinese Qigong, taught by Dr. Yan Xin. I had attended 3 major Workshops (#3, #8 and #24) and numerous other main group activities. It was at the #24 Workshop; Dr. Yan Xin taught the popular #24 steps Yang Style Tai Chi with added unique Qigong technique, which opened my mind on the Tai Chi practice. (Note: There are many variations of Yang Style Tai Chi. For instance, in the simplified Yang Style, which was standardized in China and practiced widely today, there are 24 movements). With the added Qigong method, the standard Yang style Tai Chi can be played more graceful, uniform, and a lot longer (from the usual 5-10 minutes to over 30 - 60 minutes or even longer). This is a vindication that, by adding new ingredients, the traditional martial arts can gain new vitality, which will improve its dynamics. This happens to coincide with the "Go-Tao-Chi" principle #2 - The Principle of Flow. In the Principle of Flow, it is described as "chi, motion or energy." My understanding of the "The Principle of Flow or Motion" is that it is a dynamic process, or an "ever-evolving process", where the evolution never ends. It also emphasizes that motion, action and motivation are all different perspectives of the same basic principle. In other words, how we move, what speed we move, why we move (or don't move) all are derived from the basic principle of flow.

Tai Chi movements have been taught step-by-step, throughout the years by masters in the past. A "Tai Chi system" would include bare hand boxing (Tai Chi Chuan), combat practices (Pushing Hands) as well as weapons such as Tai Chi Sword, Tai Chi Dao (Big knife), Tai Chi Staff, Tai Chi Folding Fan, etc. Each of the subsystem will have its particular forms that will require a life time practice to be considered "proper or correct," always keeping in mind the larger lessons that might be learned by the practitioner. That is what "Go-Tao-Chi" principle #3 - The Principle of Form talks about. For this book's purpose, our Tai Chi example will focus on the bare hand boxing or Tai Chi Chuan (taking into account basic body movement and kinesiology) and the general concept of chi as a foundation system, with its application and importance to Chinese medicine.

If we do a research on the Principle of Tai Chi, the Master who made Tai Chi popular in the late Chin Dynasty and was very instrumental in documenting Tai Chi principles for the modern day disciples is Chenfu Yang (1882-1935).

Let's examine some of the principles of Tai Chi movement from Master Yang's writing (excerpt from The Tai Chi Chuan Application with Diagram published by Five Continent, Taipei Taiwan 1984, pp12): "In any movement, make sure you maintain the lightness and agility of the entire body, Chi needs to be forthcoming; spirit maintains internally focused; no vulnerability, neither concave nor convex, no broken, or stoppages of movements. The root (of movement) is from the feet, transported through the legs, governed by the waist and completed by the hands and fingers. From the feet to legs to waist, the movement is fully integrated. One will gain advantage when moving forward or backward. When you lost the advantage, the most likely root cause is either in the waist or legs. Move of all directions (up/down/front/back/left/right) is based on this same principle. All these are derived from intent which is internal to oneself…"

Based on these descriptions, the typical Tai Chi movements are designed to gain advantage by disguising the real intention of the ultimate target. Therefore, it goes on saying "When you attack the upper part, the real target may be the lower part; the same with left/right. When you want to lift the opponent, by deliberately pressing him, you have induced the object to counter the pressing force, thereby lost its own center of gravity, which is the key for your gaining advantage. Always distinguish the stances (solid versus partial solid, i.e., horse stance vs. cat stance), no matter where or which part of your body is being engaged in actions. Your entire body are linked completely together, no broken area whatsoever."

Any serious Tai Chi practitioner can appreciate the above Tai Chi movement principles which are evidenced in many aspect of Tai Chi teaching and practices. These are the fundamentals, which are the basic "Form" for the "Go-Tao-Chi" principle #3 - The Principle of Form. With each individual steps of Tai Chi Chuan (postures and techniques in Five Bird Tai Chi), one needs to follow these principles to be true to Tai Chi movements and thus be able to call what they are doing "meditation in motion."

Over the past several hundred years, Tai Chi as a branch of martial arts has evolved quite a bit into today's much simplified version and styles. No doubt, it will continue to evolve, change and adapt to the current and future generations. The nature of its adaptability over time is precisely what the "Go-Tao-Chi" principle #5 calls for - the principle of "Harmony or Adaptability." For, the best systems (of martial arts, governments or techniques of teaching) are those that are not stagnant or restrictive and which can be directed toward ever shifting targets.

Biographical Note: Edward Tao was born in 1950 in Taipei, Taiwan. He came to U.S. for his graduate study in 1976, with a Master in Industrial Engineering in 1978 from Auburn University; and later in 1983 a MBA degree from University of Toledo. Through most of his working careers, Ed has been working in the Automotive / Manufacturing Industries as a quality consultant (Omnex, Apex Consulting), Director of Quality (Ultra Motor, Arvin Meritor, Dana), Supplier Quality Manager (Tenneco Automotive), Quality Systems Manager, Manufacturing / Quality Manager, Senior Industrial Engineer and Manufacturing Engineer. Ed's lifetime interests include: Martial Arts; Qigong; Tennis, Golfing, reading and traveling. This article was originally written in his second language of English (the form you see here), and later translated back into Chinese.

The Five Birds System

By Rick Burgin

When is a martial arts style really a style? What makes a fighter a martial artist? And, what do we call a style that is founded entirely on ideas? The answer to these and other intriguing questions are attracting more and more people to a fairly new, but traditionally taught form of martial arts called, The Five Bird System.

Concept Training—

"What attracted me to the Five Bird System is the way that I was taught," says Karl Goldschmidt, three year student of Gordon Richiusa's Five Bird System, eclectic martial arts with a very specific focus: training martial artists.

To accomplish this elusive task, The Five Bird System focuses on the student's individual needs, boils almost everything down to its five component parts and emphasizes a simplified teaching method it calls Concept Training. This form of training acknowledges the usual Mind, Body and Spirit triangle of most martial arts. But, the mind and the body are considered separate entities that can be taught separately and even progress at different rates. Here the student can be grilled in the reasons WHY they are learning a technique, long before they actually know what the technique IS.

"I like the way that students are constantly challenging themselves to answer questions. It's like being a part of the experiment, but you already have the solution. The questions you ask and the answers that you get are often given to us out of order. For instance," adds Karl," we're usually asked 'how many?' of this or how many parts are there of that. We're told in our very first lesson that the answer is almost always five. So, we start off just giving the answer like robots. Eventually we're forced to think about the questions and understand the meaning of what we're saying."

Gordon Richiusa, director and founder of the Five Bird System admits that his method of teaching is as old as Socrates, in that it continuously draws the correct response from the student, both physically and mentally by creating an inner dialogue. "That is the traditional part of what I do. I'm not afraid to admit that I rely heavily on what truly great thinkers and martial artists have said before me. That's why my techniques don't look, merely like the traditional Goju-ryu that is the karate foundation of what I teach. A Jujitsu person will see what we do and, maybe, call it jujitsu. A kung fu person sees similarities with their art, while I've also heard comparisons from people originally in Hap Ki Do, Kempo, Isshinryu and even Tai Chi."

There's a reason for this phenomenon. Five Birds Concepts are based upon the central idea that all styles have similarities and that the similarities are all that we should be concerned with. It's not that all styles are all really the same. Many of Gordon's students, in fact, have earned rank, and come to him from other styles. Some have gone on to other forms AFTER studying with Gordon. "Each style emphasizes some specific aspect or concept, but all are really trying to accomplish the same objectives, be it self defense, self discipline, self awareness or a combination of those. "Our goal," explains Wes Cotton, 15 year student of the Five Bird System and senior instructor." As teachers of martial arts, is to present ideas and situations in the most memorable and exciting ways. I came to Gordon with experience in kenpo. He never held that against me, but emphasized it as an advantage. So, now, as a teacher, if I have to sway from Goju and revert to an explanation that I heard in a kenpo class to make my points, it's O.K. Gordon did the same thing to me!"

The Five Bird System uses the traditional Okinawan karate style of Goju Kai as a foundation, but also teaches a number of weapons including Kyudo (archery), bo and jo-do (long and short staff technique), escrima, shaken and shuriken throwing (including tomahawks), and kenjutsu (swordsmanship), as well as a number of survival-arts (climbing, edible plant identification, tracking). The Five Bird System has been around for 25 years, but it is only recently that Gordon has begun to put labels on his techniques and teaching methods. "Gordon has studied, earned rank at and taught for many different studios and styles, "explains Brian Wallace, a friend and student of Gordon's for the past thirteen years. "He's been in the martial arts for 36 years, but, he's always considered his methods, just as a way of teaching, rather than a style of its own."

As more and more people began devoting their time to learning what Gordon had to teach, the Five Bird System began to take shape. "From the beginning of my training, I was introduced to various other teachers who all had specialties if their own that they wanted to share. None of the specialties ever seemed to have much to do with karate, but all held fast to similar convictions. More importantly, each of the teachers who I held in high regard all had other authorities, myths and legends that they quoted and submitted to. After a while, the legends and stories started to become my teachers, which was the whole point, I believe. I was told how this or that master had observed nature and deduced scientific principles. I was told to observe nature in the same way as the masters did. By following this example, I became part of a larger picture, long before I could actually perform at a level of efficiency. Eventually, a transformation came about without me really knowing it. All I had to do was trust my teachers and submit to the belief that the training would eventually make everything clear."

"In The Five Bird System," explains Gordon; "we understand that a student must be led along, almost tricked into learning, since the bottom line is that learning to internalize technique requires years of hard work. Almost no one would begin such a journey if you told him or her that you couldn't explain what it was they were really going to learn and that the training would never really end. So, to trick the body, the mind is kept active with catchy phrases, advice, stories, puzzles and questions. This occupies it just long enough for the body to catch up to it. Then, we make sure that what we believe to be true IS true, by examining the results against what countless others who have called themselves martial artists have believed before us. When something checks out, then it is repeated again and again. We even use the same words over and over, until they can be recited and even elaborated upon."

The whole process, according to Gordon is nothing more than anyone should expect from a good student-teacher relationship. That is why the Five Bird System calls itself the first Student Oriented Style, and also why it borrows liberally from just about every other art and science.

"To be a good teacher you should know your subject, of course," explains Gordon. "But you also need to find ways to make the lessons interesting and memorable. I can get anyone to throw a perfect kick... one time. The trick is getting their minds and their bodies to remember how to do it later and for the rest of their lives. Then, I let them in on the secret, that what I really want to get them to see is that punching and kicking are very limited skills, in the end. If that's all we end up learning in a martial arts class, then we've really wasted out time."

Why Five? Five is an essential number in many martial arts forms (five senses, five animals, five powers, five strategies of Sun Tzu and the five positions of Miyamoto Musashi) and it is the number to remember in the Five Bird System. The five birds (eagle, owl, hawk, vulture, raven) represent not only individual characteristics, strategies and goals, but are each, essential parts of the whole, and there is more.

"Like the different types of fighting, the Five Birds all have very different ways of surviving. However, they all have one primary thing in common. They all fly! They are all successful even within their limitations; they all have strengths and weaknesses. The Eagle is a metaphor for grappling technique, Spirit and the ability to use our sight. The Hawk represents speed and triangulation and has great Courage. The Owl is a very basic bird. Its survival is based upon simple Skill. It sits in a tree and waits for dinner to come to it! One swift, silent move is all it needs. Therefore, it also teaches us about camouflage and the sense of hearing. From the Vulture we learn a warrior's humility or Honor, how to use multiple weapons and the sense of smell. The Raven represents Adaptability, a willingness to throw out technique. It's a bird that brings together all the other strategies, but never quite masters any of them. It's also the only bird, which performs its real maneuvers purely for the fun of it. It's a lot of people."

The Way to What

So, since every fighting style can have weaknesses, knowledge of the weaknesses can be invaluable. But, what of the similarities? Along these lines, one of the first lessons Five Bird students are given is an explanation of the word Dojo. As with every aspect of Five Bird Concept Training, all information is of equal importance and all arts are treated with equal respect. However, behind every small bit of training, there is an underlying, larger, concept that is trying to reach the student. Sometimes, even the teacher doesn't know what the larger concept is. As long as the student approaches the training with an open mind, body and spirit, then the framework for enlightenment is already built and in place. The lessons are all around us. All we have to do is unravel their meaning. "It can be a problem to get too hung up on definitions though," says Gordon. "I have been in numerous heated conversations about whether I studied Goju Ryu or Goju Kai. Teachers can get really hung up on technicalities. To me, what difference does it make?"

In the case of the word, Dojo, Gordon had this to say, "Literally translated the word "do" (pronounced dough) denotes a thing as The Way. Karate-do is the way through the learning of karate, or empty hand technique. Ken-do, is the way of the blade. Bu-do is the way of the warrior.

The suffix "jo" is a word that designates a place. So, Dojo, literally means, the place of the way, or the place where one goes to learn The Way. The question almost always arises at this point, the way to WHAT? If a student asks this question, then I know he's got potential, because he's using his best weapon...his brain. If he or she doesn't ask this question, then I ask it for them." It is invaluable, in The Five Bird System, to understand the importance of "little things" because, the ability to answer questions, in essence, is the dividing point between what denotes a martial art from that which is merely fighting technique.

Therefore, the most fundamentally important thing for a student to know about a style that they are thinking of devoting years of study to is whether it IS a way to something, or if they are just going to learn about fighting. "If a person wants to learn to fight, I recommend going into a hard neighborhood and start picking fights. In this way, if they survive, they WILL learn to fight. They will also save me a lot of time and themselves some money, and probably get a few bad scars and memories."

Simply put, this idea is that we train in martial arts, with diligence, because we are really trying to attain a special enlightenment or understanding. There are plenty of good fighters out there who are really NOT martial artists at all.

Why? It is because there is no soul, no point to their training. In my method, we begin with the intent to embark on a path ... The Way. If that desire is not there, then a student must go some other place to study. I don't teach fighting, although good fighting technique will certainly be a bi-product of this path. I teach in the same, traditional manner that I was taught. I teach martial arts as a way of life, as a way of improving ones view of his or her place and purpose. Anything attempted in this vein can achieve the same benefits. It doesn't even have to be a martial art. But, martial arts are what I know, so that is at the core of what I teach.

Anything is Better Than Nothing

One of the most important concepts in Five Bird System is *anything is better than nothing.*

To demonstrate the application of this principle Gordon uses a number of methods, but one of the more colorful and memorable is when he ties up a new student and then directs them to escape. Usually, he says, a student will just freeze and say that they can't, because they've never been taught HOW to escape from a tangle of ropes. Gordon, or one of the other Five Birds teachers, will then direct the student to "Think about this for a moment" and teach them how to get out of their bindings, while leading them through the process that they will need to perfect in the rest of the training. Phrases they might hear during this process will include:

1) What are you trying to accomplish? Always keep sight of your actual goal.

2) There are strengths and weaknesses in our opponent and ourselves.

3) If the rope is your opponent, what are the holes in the opposition?

4) Don't forget, anything is better than nothing.

"All of our lessons are geared toward making a point. In the case of tying people up, the point comes as we direct them on what to do next. Because, really, the small points or concepts, are what all martial arts are about. In the case of the ropes, we can see precisely what we are trying to do is to get the ropes off. The opposition is simple, in a sense. No matter how tangled the ropes might appear, they really only do one thing. The ropes are kind of a physical metaphor for those styles that think they have the secret. With the ropes, there are holes every place that they make contact with you. When you're tied up with a long rope, all you have to do is loosen one spot. When you do this, the rest of the rope also loosens. But, if you do nothing at all, then the ropes remain tight. You don't really have to know HOW to fight the ropes. Any movement will eventually loosen them. Anything, in this case, is better than nothing. Time after time, we show how this kind of attitude will make the difference between success and failure."

The Brain is the Best Weapon

This, another vital Five Birds concept has two main aspects. To illustrate the first, Gordon entertains the students with a story that deals with him when he was just entering high school. "I went to a really rough school, racially mixed and, unfortunately, very volatile. Everyone was looking for trouble. And, this was at a time, when gangs and groups were becoming necessary to survive." On the first day of school, a large group of older kids who Gordon describes as, "about thirty in number" surrounded each, new, unfortunate kid as they walked into school. "I was one of those unfortunate kids, and I suddenly found myself surrounded by thirty opponents, asking for my lunch money and threatening me with physical harm. I had been training to in karate for several years and I thought I was pretty good. But, instead of fighting, luckily, I had a moment of true wisdom and a totally different kind of strategy came to mind. I began reciting Shakespeare! I did a scene from Romeo and Juliet, that rambles on about love and ends with the line, "*What is it else? A madness most discreet, a choking gull, preserving sweet, farewell my Cos.*" And, I used that opportunity to walk right through the middle of them and get away. No body moved; they were spellbound and baffled by my performance."

The story continues in that the next day, he saw the crowd gathering again, ready to surround him, but instead of asking for money, somebody called out. 'Hey, it's the crazy guy! Do some of that Shakespeare stuff for us.'

"I had to learn a lot of scenes from different plays, but I never lost my lunch money to robbers. Eventually, I was an honorary member of several different clubs. It was kind of like being a mascot, like being the village idiot. It was taboo to bother me, because I was just too weird."

What did Gordon get from all this? "Be willing to abandon technique! Creativity is its own reward and there is a particular power in words." Later, this kind of thinking translated into one of the five basic strategies for overcoming an opponent: Change The Game and became the focus of Gordon's interest in creative writing.

This also relates to a common mistake in many styles which Gordon calls being Weapon Stupid. We all learn to accept the premise that knowledge is power. In a direct, one-on-one confrontation, the truth in this statement can take on immediate and tangible meaning, even something as simple as making a fist. "I've heard people trash Tae Kwon Do fighters as ineffective, but I've known some very effective fighters from that style. I've also seen people dazzled with kicks that could easily be defended against, IF the defender had only seen such a kick before."

In other words, people often forget exactly what they are trying to accomplish and concentrate their attentions in the wrong area. This is true when the hands are empty OR when they are holding something, but the principle is the same. Don't rely on any one weapon and don't try to play the other guys game. In the middle of the fight is not a good time to be impressed with your opponents kicking height, or the fact the he has a knife and you don't. Concentrate on fighting the person and be willing to "let go of your sword" as Musashi put it. If you have a favorite weapon and it is rendered useless, you need a back-up plan. Realize that an attacker who brandishes his weapons against you is trying to use a threat factor and your ignorance in his favor.

Many times, if you can knock a weapon away from a person, or simply take control of it, the person will concentrate all of his or her efforts on restoring the weapon! That's being weapon stupid. The weapon cannot hurt you. If you are attacked, use your best weapon and fight the person, with whatever weapons you have available."

Defense Awareness

So, what should the end result of martial arts training be, according to the Five Bird System? "When people ask, 'the Way to What?' The Five Bird System has a modern, ready-made answer: Defense Awareness is part of a Successful Life Strategy.

"Defense Awareness is a concept based in the understanding that every style, just as every individual, has strengths as well as weaknesses. Therefore, the only conflict that a person can guarantee they'll come away from victorious is one that they never have to fight. It also deals with the difference between paranoia and Applied Awareness, one of the basic principles of Chi"

Discovering your Successful Life Strategy is based upon the belief, first of all, that one exists. It also emphasizes that having real success means something MORE than just getting more than the other guy. To find the answer in our own lives about what is success, we look at what it is that all people are really trying to obtain. The answer is Happiness. "No matter what people may be trying to accomplish, it all boils down to simple happiness," says Gordon. "And, there is a difference between happiness and pleasure. Happiness is a simple, basic human goal that sustains us throughout a lifetime. Pleasure is brief and shallow. That doesn't mean that happiness can't have moments of pleasure. But, if we strive for pleasure, then we will on achieve that shallow goal. A successful life strategy is a plan that is easy to follow, that NO ONE has to suffer for."

Every style also has something else in common, and that is strengths and weaknesses. No style is any better, or worse than the practitioner's dedication to perfection or his ability to carry out his strategies. The Five Bird System emphasizes the interrelationship of things, natural laws and geometry.

For instance, when a Five Birds teacher shows you a technique, they never stop there. They also show you alternatives and variations, as well as the weaknesses and strengths of the technique. "After all, someone may use the technique on you someday. Then what?"

There are at least two perspectives from which to view every conflict. Not only do you need to know your own possible options in a situation, but to make an educated decision on choosing a strategy, you should also take into account what your opponent is capable of. "Knowledge becomes power at every turn," says Gordon. "If I know that my opponent's fist is not tight enough to hurt me and will actually cause him damage, then, instead of blocking, I might prefer to let his fist land. Knowledge of a good fist over a bad one can be the advantage in this type of encounter."

What the Five Bird System tries to do is boil things down to their essence, make an impact with the teaching and the techniques by always allowing the individual room to experiment and grow. In this way, the Five Birds System is merely a way of teaching the larger principles of martial arts, in general. The focus then is taken away from the techniques and is centered on helping the student become the best person they can be in every conceivable situation.

Five Parts of A Self Defense Technique

No matter what technique you do, there are always five parts that must be accomplished. By the way, Frank Dux has his FASST system, which emphasizes these steps and the term FASST is an acronym for his system. Since I was a student of Frank Dux for many years, it's not unusual that there would be this overlap. So, in Five Birds Martial Arts we say that first, you must Defend Yourself; often this is accomplished with a block or deflection of the initial attack. Second, we say that you must *lower your center of gravity*. Third, for a successful defense, a defender must do a Break Up. This is the moment when the defender turns the tables on the attacker, no longer accepting the defensive role. Fourth, there is the moment when one must Take Control.

And, finally, there is the Finish. This is the moment when we know that the initial attack has been nullified and is no longer a threat, a moment when it is over.

"Even in a basic block and counter technique," explains Gordon. "If you are going to be successful and do it right, you must defend yourself. Your center of gravity is lowered every time you go into a good stance, and EVEN falling correctly IS a self-defense technique, because there is active participation. You must also reverse the role of victim/attacker. That is what we call a break-up.

"This could be as simple as grabbing the other guy back, yelling loudly or striking. It changes the complexion of an attack, regardless. Many times, these first three parts come at exactly the same moment. Then, a point comes when you've got control, either a hold, you've outrun the other guy or your initial strike has been effective. Now, YOU decide how to end the attack, or a new situation emerges, such as a second punch, the whole process begins again."

The ancient martial artists and strategists did not invent their styles and ideas randomly. They observed nature and a human's place in the scheme of things. The skills they learned proved effective in some way. They did what they did, and said what they said, because of the conditions that presented themselves at the time of the training. Some people make fun of traditional technique, but no matter how much different we try to believe we've become, we are basically, still the same human beings.

Our hands and feet still only move in the same ways and our universe is made up of only two geometric shapes...straight lines and curved ones. I believe that the laws of Newton and Einstein would make sense to the ancients if we could have explained these to them. Einstein's theory of energy conversion from mass and speed is true now just as it was BEFORE we knew what it meant. The amount of energy a thing, a weapon, a fist, a foot can generate is based upon speed and mass. Move something very small, but fast enough, you can generate great energy. The ancient masters' words, to me, are like the books in a large oral library. Books don't get into a library because they are worthless, and the masters did not teach, or learn, worthless technique. If we look at all individual perspective and technique on this larger scale, then there is something valuable to be learned from every person willing to tell you what they think! This is especially true, if they tell us WHY they think it."

The Five Principles of Successful Business Practice

By Steve Galvanoni

(Note: This information has been disseminated, in more or less detailed form to every client of ETC. The information below also makes up the bulk of many of Steve Galvanoni's workshops on successful business. We would like to acknowledge a special gratitude to Mr. Galvanoni for sharing this very valuable essay with us.)

In the Business Vision of ETC there are what is called **Business Drivers.** These include *Financial Strength*, which relates to Growth (Revenue & Profitability), *Expansion* (Mergers & Acquisitions), *Operational Performance* (SG&A), and *Risk Management*. Another Driver is *Product Portfolio*. With Product Portfolio we have *Core Competencies* (Products & Services), *Brand Awareness* (Mind Share, Customer Service Competitiveness), and *New Product Development*. Another driver that needs consideration is the *Delivery Channels* which includes Group Shared Service Operations, Facilities & Operations, Electronic (e and c) Services, Consumer Care Centers and Business Customers. The final business driver is *Customer*

Services with Consumer Value Proposition (Market Share), Marketing/Advertising, and Member Service Responsiveness.

While focusing on business drivers one must also consider Information Technology Drivers, as Information Technology is a dynamic that can affect the success of the operation. **Without going into detail, the five essential considerations are summarily listed as People, Product, Process, Platform and Partners.**

The perspective we utilize is called Strategic Information Systems Planning Solution Approach. First is the Enterprise Level Assessment, where the question "Where are you today?" is asked. Secondly, we apply a Strategic Solution Definition, which ultimately–taking into consideration your strengths and weaknesses, your assets and liabilities—asks another question, "What should you look like?" Thirdly, after analyzing the situation and determining what you are ultimately trying to accomplish, ETC will help you make a Solution Delivery Selection, which basically asks the final question, "What is your best solution and how do you get there?"

My name is Steve Galvanoni; I'm CEO of ETC. Previously I spent 25 plus years in my business career associated with barcodes, scanning and mobile computing systems. My experience in business has allowed me to understand the Five Principles in this way: The first principle is Applied Awareness, which has to do with answering the question, 'What do you want to accomplish?' I was involved in the initial stages of inventing the barcode and what we wanted to accomplish was with the grocery manufacturers of America and Supermarket Institute is a unique marking system for consumer package goods that allow traceability and the ability of scanning these particular barcodes for informational purposes. The second principle is that of Benefit. In this case we wanted to provide information that would be a benefit to or for the retailer or the individual system so that we could then see particular movement in certain categories in s store, unique to that individual item. There were many ways to accomplish the gathering of that information as time went on, which deals with our third principle of for m. We started off with the barcode symbology that is associated with capturing data and moved on to multiple types of different barcodes including the UPC code, to a 2 D barcode. Today, as well as with RFID or tag technology this provides a significant amount of information with no human intervention. We also take into account, as with the principle of Flow, that the Business Universe does not stand still but is in continual motion. That's very true as it relates to the technology of mobile and barcode scanning.

If you look in the past at Moore's Law with the formation of Intel, you will see that memory for devices are incrementally increased significantly over a short period of time. Also you'll see that, just by the example of the different types of methodologies of barcoding, these technologies have advanced significantly. Last but not least we are looking at the harmony, or balance of all the technology. This is very important, because when you apply technology to people you must have technologies that are easily understood, so that they can be adaptable. In today's world, the intermediation of smart phones and other technologies that allow you to get instant information, anytime, anyplace to anyone anywhere in near real time sub-second response time has certainly made the world a smaller place to live from a communications standpoint.

What you are going to see, in my opinion, in the future is the continued evolution of these types of technologies that will be rapidly deployed to improve and provide better information for businesspeople to make informed decisions in a real time nature.

Today's world moves rapidly. We are constantly barraged by information and clutter daily, hourly, minute-by-minute, second-by-second with new delivery systems and technologies such as cellphones, texting, Twitter and other social media. Do you remember the first technologies that brought about this change? It was pagers. But, at least with pagers you still had enough control over the situation to ignore a page if you wanted to, until you were ready to respond to it. I believe that with the rapid technological advancements it's creating societal problems and interruptions during times that put us on notice for work or social engagements, twenty-four hours a day, seven days a week. This is not healthy in my opinion. There has to be times when we, as individuals are able to step away from everything, shut off our devices, including televisions and just think, relax and do what we want to do, without being beholden to a device or responsible to give an instant answer to somebody. If you consider what you want in life, which is success or significance, it's paramount to determine what's important in life, and how you are going to live your life. When you make a plan, structure it in a manner that meets your goals and objectives and determine whether you want success or significance. I believe you can have both, but the success has to be in moderation.

A video version of Steve Galvanoni's statement appears as a Message In A Bottle, on YouTube and www.vision-revision.pbwiki.com

Conservative Values and The Five Principles Everything

By Dana Stamos

I consider myself a *conservative* based on my adherence to the following guiding principles: I respect the Constitution; I respect human life; I believe in small Government and I believe in personal responsibility and accountability. I was asked how I felt my conservative viewpoint fit with the Five Principles of Everything.

The Five Principles of Everything, are difficult to discuss because they are very broad, all encompassing. For the sake of focus, I defined them for this article as:

- The Principle of Awareness - The way we think and feel about something affects our actions.
- The Principle of Flow - What moves us will motivate our actions.

- The Principle of Form - There are different ways to accomplish the same goal.
- The Principle of Benefit - Does what we have chosen to do accomplish our goal, or have a payoff?
- The Principle of Harmony - If we are not accomplishing our goal, or if any of the principles are being violated, can we change what we are doing or should we change the goal?

Having grown up in a very politically active and conservative home, I was often the subject of negative comments about conservatives from others of different political persuasions. One of the comments I heard most often was "Conservatives don't care about people, only about the bottom line." As with any generalization, this could be true about anyone from any political persuasion, and it is definitely not true about me, or my conservative beliefs. In fact, I believe my conservative views fit extremely well within the framework of the 5 Principles of Everything.

For the purpose of this article, let's choose one issue, social welfare, and look at it from a traditionally conservative perspective. I firmly believe that one of the highest examples of human awareness can be found in a desire to *serve one another*. In short, we are here on Earth to "love our neighbors as ourselves." How we accomplish this is the *form* our actions take to demonstrate an awareness of this universal goal. However, by the same token, the “way” we serve is not as important as the awareness that service is important. We must also make sure that our method of service and even the definition of it doesn’t violate any of the other basic principles. This means that while we may want to meet one another's needs, we also might want to hold one another accountable to be the most productive citizens possible. It’s human nature to want others to *take responsibility* for *their lives*, as much as you feel *you* take responsibility for *your* life. This often requires "tough love,” not a favorite concept for many of us.

By virtue of the importance we place on Awareness, it seems logical if we are to love one another, then we must actually *know* one another. Only then can we be aware of one another's needs. Then, and only then, can we respond with necessary actions that will truly make a difference. "Let the man with two tunics share with him who has none, and let him who has food do likewise."

In other words, while we should be concerned with everyone’s welfare, the current welfare system does not meet the five principle test. Within the current system, some pay taxes and their money goes to Washington D.C.; We often don’t see where the money is going, and therefore can turn a blind eye the needs of our fellow humans. There is no immediate and obvious motivation to help those we don't see. For those who don't see the Bigger Picture, it is no longer a responsibility to take action within our community; it is now *the Government's* responsibility. (We don't have to be Aware or personally responsible). We, as individuals and as families, are no longer our "brother's keeper." Thus, the social welfare bureaucracy becomes completely impersonal and simply throws money at the problem, with substandard results and little or no individual accountability. (No Lasting Benefit).

Within the framework of social conservatism, small government means that our tax dollars stay within the communities and are used to help individuals within our communities. When towns were small, this was easier. The people living in the towns knew one another and met one another's needs. As conservatives, we want to see that our tax dollars are spent as close to home as possible, that funding stays in our towns to be used by those who know the needs of the people of our town, not sent to Washington D.C. and doled out by a bureaucracy without a clue about the needs of neighborhoods. We want to be involved in the process along with our neighbors, and we can be involved if the process takes place in the observable place where we live. The problem is that we are also living in a much wider *community* than is apparent.

It would be nice to step back to the small town mentality where neighbors looked out for one another. If we care for our neighbors, those who we actually talk to on a daily basis, then we will be aquatinted with their needs, and also with their habits. We will have a relationship with them and will be just as responsible for helping them to become productive citizens as we are with helping to cloth and feed them. We will not want to play into bad habits, but instead we will see the whole person, and determine what their needs really are. If a person is offered a job and doesn't take it, because it is easier to use the income of others, we will know this and respond accordingly. (*"If a man will not work, he shall not eat.")* If a woman consistently has children out of wedlock that she cannot support, she needs mentoring and not just a Welfare Check. This approach requires citizens to be dedicated to helping others within our own communities and it means giving, not just tax dollars, but our personal time and talents to make a difference. In the long run, the benefits are higher, not just for those receiving help, but for those who are giving the help as well.

I am a conservative, and I believe that my conservative values seek to promote smaller government, but larger hearts, more responsibility and accountability, and less Washington intervention. I also think that having this opinion about *how* to accomplish a universal goal—one that might be different from others who label themselves differently—is what The Five Principles are all about, finding common ground for solving problems and establishing order. I think that the Constitution of the United States of America, as the Five Principles seem to be, are more about seeking this common footing than about arguing our differences.

The Principle of Awareness - We see the problem up close and personal.

The Principle of Flow - We are moved to action by what we see.

The Principle of Form - We find the very best solutions to solve the issues.

The Principle of Benefit - We make sure we have the most beneficial solution for all.

The Principle of Harmony - When it isn't working, we are willing to change and to search for new solutions.

Dana Stamos is the publisher of WorldWideDojo.com and USAdojo.com. Her writings reach hundreds of thousands of readers annually.

Op/Ed Writing and the Five Principles of Everything

By Russ Buchanan

I write about politics…by *choice*. Why a relatively well-adjusted guy would involve himself in such a demented business as American politics is difficult for many to understand — myself included. But politics hooked me as a teenager and for forty years has refused to let me go. As soon as it does, though… I'm going to get a life.

As a politics hound, I am frequently in the position of trying to persuade readers who disagree with me to see the "error of their ways." Often, this is a fool's errand because most political beliefs are shaped by the reader's worldview and set in stone. But every once in a while, my words reach into a reader's brain and dislodge a firmly held "truth" or two, or at least my words get that reader to rethink his position. Those admittedly rare but wonderful, "gee, I never thought about it that way" letters and emails are like manna from heaven to me and remind me of why I write about politics. They tell me my writing can make a difference.

Political writing is an idiosyncratic business. From the very conservative style of very conservative George Will of the *Post* to the verbal pyrotechnics of *Rolling Stone's* "Gonzo" journalist, the late Hunter S. Thompson, the styles are as varied as the writers' personalities. However, there are conventions and methods helpful to all writers, regardless of their style. The Five Principles of Everything is just such an aid.

Consulting the Principles heightens my awareness of the issue, improves my argument and increases the chance of me getting through to the opposition. The Principles help clarify arguments; they also separate the lean from the fat, the ego-driven from the pertinent and the silly from the serious. In other words, used as a five-point checklist, the Principles help make my piece ready for prime time.

Principle of Benefit—When I sit down at the computer to carve out an essay, it is important that I understand why I'm making the argument in the first place — or as the Principle of Benefit puts it, "what's in it for me?" If I'm arguing to boost my ego, personally dominate or humiliate the opposition, impress everybody with my devastating wit or any reasons other than educating, conveying opinion and/or attempting to persuade, then I should go take a nap instead.

Principle of Flow—Ever since we crawled out of the swamp, we've been telling stories to each other. In fact, the very first story was probably a first proto-person account of getting out of that miserable swamp. As natural storytellers and listeners, we expect information to move, or *flow*. My articles are designed to take the reader on a mini-journey, with a beginning, middle and ending. If I've done my job right, my argument's unwritten epilogue will be the movement of my readers — to vote, to contribute money or time, or simply to tell their friends about the new, "enlightened" way they view the candidate or issue.

Principles of Form and Harmony—The *form* of my argument must fit — or be in *harmony* with — my readership/audience. Accordingly, the principles of Form and Harmony are inextricably linked in my writing. For example, the words and references I use when writing for a general readership are quite different from those I would use for a group of political activists.

My tone must also be in harmony with the topic itself. For instance, I like to inject a little humor into my work now and then — but only when *appropriate*. Tossing a couple "hilarious" riffs into a piece about AIDS or the death penalty would not only siphon gravitas from the subject matter but would also make me look like a stone-hearted jerk.

Op/ed writers who maintain a one-style-fits-all approach to writing risk alienating their readership by writing above or below their understanding level, writing inappropriately or committing the worst offense of all: *boring* everybody.

The Principle of Applied Awareness—In politics, a duck is often not a duck. In fact, that poor duck can emerge as anything from a finch to a pterodactyl, depending on the spin. It is my job to be *aware* of the opposing viewpoint, to wade through all of the pretense, political correctness and superfluous adornment to get to the *real* reason he feels the way he does — and attack it without mercy, of course.

Without that clear understanding of "*the way [they] think and feel about*" an issue, any hope of persuading the readers goes out the window.

The Principles In Practice—A November 2011 poll by the Pew Research Center found Americans nearly equally divided on the issue of gay marriage — 46% in favor - 44% opposed. How I would formulate an essay on this divisive issue offers insight into the Five Principles of Everything in action.

Awareness—Rule #1: If the opposition is religious, forget it. Nothing I can write will change the reader's mind. In fact, what I write would no doubt be interpreted as an attack on his religion, rendering me forever a minion of Satan and someone who is wrong about everything.

However, many oppose gay marriage for another reason: plain old, secular, garden-variety intolerance. Although some really believe gay marriage will undermine traditional marriage/family and lead to polygamy and other more exotic assignations, I believe many others know that there isn't a shred of evidence supporting those fears and merely use those reasons as convenient excuses to mask the politically incorrect bigotry they feel toward the LGBT community. For the most part, these are not haters or inherently bad people; they simply don't understand homosexuality and feel threatened by it.

Am I *aware* of how my readers think and feel about gay marriage? Check.

Form and Harmony—When I write about gay marriage/rights, I *form* my arguments to be in *harmony* with this particular group of readers. Though they are opposed to same-sex marriage, I believe their fair-mindedness and common sense will respond positively to the argument that homosexuality is an un-chosen phenomenon. "Who would *choose* such a difficult path in life?" I ask. "Do you really think teenagers enjoy getting beaten up after school or look enthusiastically forward to the day they'll tell their parents not to expect grandchildren from them?" "Are you really going to punish this large segment of the American population for something they had absolutely no control over?" Questions like these put the lie to homosexuality as an intentional, naughty flaunting of our moral code and appeal to my readers' as fair and compassionate human beings. I might also zero in on my readers' emotions by pointing out the deleterious effects of discrimination and marginalization, such as the incredibly high suicide rates among gay youth. I may even throw in a few words about bigotry being un-American and unconstitutional for the patriots in the group.

That my work on gay marriage/rights is responsible for more of those glorious "aha moment" letters from readers than any other tells me that my *form* has been in *harmony* with my readers on more than a few occasions.

Is my *form* in *harmony* with my readers and the subject matter? Check.

Flow—Writing about gay marriage/rights doesn't pose any special consideration regarding movement or flow. As with all of my writing, I just make sure that the piece has continuity and that it moves along, with a beginning, middle and end.

Of course, I hope my writing moves many opinions from the "against" column to the "for" column. But, believe me; I'd be satisfied with a nice little note from a reader telling me that my article made him rethink his position on this gay marriage business.

Does the piece *flow*? Check.

Is it designed to *move* my readers? Check.

Benefit—The issue of gay rights puts my blood pressure in the stratosphere. In my humble, extremely biased opinion, the sheer unfairness of denying rights to a large group of Americans based on their sexual orientation is cruel, narrow-minded, and extremely un-American. The personal benefit I hope to derive from any writing I do on the subject might be the knowledge that I helped end a maddening and immoral discrimination, and shouldn't we also consider the benefit that is being derived by any person who can share a feeling of love with another?

As an Op-Ed columnist, I know I need to look at every question from as many angles, as possible, to *write a good column.* From the Five Principles perspective I must also keep in mind universal principles. In the end, I ask myself if I am writing for the right *benefits* and make sure that no one else's benefits are being violated. If the answer is yes, in both cases then check/check.

Conclusion—In all the above, if we somehow forget that no one principle, or our interpretation of it is the actual goal—Remember that all five principles work together like fingers on a glove— then we might get caught up in a fruitless argument about a fine point, and miss the broad strokes. For instance, if one believes that sex is only for procreation or that there is no real value in simply loving and being loved, beyond our ability to have children, then The Big Picture argument is out the window. Politics is a sometimes frustrating, often confusing, always exciting struggle. Writing about politics is all that and carpal tunnel syndrome too. All things considered, there's nothing else I'd rather be doing. As a political writer, I sit ringside, observing the greatest democracy the world has ever known in all its beautiful craziness and then I get to tell people about it. Thanks to the Five Principles of Everything, I am able to do that *better*.

Russ Buchanan is a successful and talented voice-over actor, musician and composer. One of his popular video parodies All American Suckers *appears on Vision-Revision (with permission). His music is available through all the usual sources, and his writing can be found at the online magazine,* Midnight Graffiti *and his own political blog,* Craving Sense*: http://russellbuchanan.wordpress.com*

The Tao of Teaching or Learning as Meditation

By Brian Wallace

I am honored to be asked by Gordon Richiusa to write down a few thoughts of how martial arts relates to education and educational systems. I am not sure I am the best person to write on the subject, but will do my best.

I have worked in education for the past twenty-five years. In that time I have been a teacher, mentor teacher, Technology Director, and currently Executive Director Operations for a mid-sized school district in the Pacific NW. I have developed curriculum, taught at the college level, and have served on State-Wide Commissions. I also serve on the Board of Trustees of my resident school district.

I am also one of Gordon's Black Belt students. My journey to earn my black belt showed me that martial artists are the best teachers. As I continued my career in education, it became very clear that the principles of excellent martial arts instruction are the same principles that excellent teachers, schools, and school systems follow. The terminology used may be difference, but the principals are universal.

Education, at its best, is very Zen like. It is the process, not the result. As martial artists, we understand this. For example, if I have a student who is interested in breaking, I do not have the student start pounding boards and bricks. We work on speed, form, focus, and trauma training (toughening up the body). Why? Because I know that a student who has excellent form, speed, and focus will generate a tremendous amount of power. Breaking boards will not be a problem.

So how does this fit into an educational system, which (at least for the past decade) is completely focused on high-stakes testing? It is actually fairly simple. We can't focus on the results of those standardized tests. To be excellent, schools and school districts must concentrate on improving their professional practice and the art and science of teaching. Not an easy task. Educational systems are dynamic and complex. Individuals in the system are pulled in many directions. Politics, special interests, and hidden agendas often get in the way of systematic improvement, but it can be done.

My local school district is a high achieving district. 90% of students are meeting or exceeding State standards at all levels. However, looking at the demographics of the district, you would not expect such a high rate of success. 60% of the enrolled students qualify for Free and Reduced lunch in the National School Lunch Program. The percentage of parents with a bachelor's degree or higher is only 11%. This is significantly lower than our State and National averages. Neighboring districts with higher household incomes do not score as high. Why is our local school district doing so well? I asked the Superintendent of Schools. *"We hire the best teachers we can find. We make sure they do not work in isolation. Our curriculum is aligned to the State Standards and teachers adjust instruction to meet individual needs. Grades reflect what a student knows and are never used as a form of punishment. What we do here is not magic, but a process of continuous improvement."*

My first reaction to this was, "Sounds good, nice talking points, but is this happening at the classroom level? Has this philosophy moved from the central office and embraced by the whole organization?" My questions were answered a couple of weeks later.

I was attending a Board of Directors Meeting and part of the agenda was a presentation by one of our high school principals. The presentation focused on changes with the school's math instruction, state assessments, and SAT/ACT scores. During the presentation, one of my fellow Board members asked, "How will the changes help to prepare our students for the High School Exit exam?"

The principal replied, (and I paraphrase), "We are in the middle of a fundamental change in how we teach. We truly are focused on our instruction, keeping classes interesting, and making sure kids learn. This is a big change from the way we taught 15-20 years ago. In the past, if a student was failing a course, the teacher usually assigned more homework. If that did not work, then the student failed. The student always had the option of repeating the subject and, ironically, the opportunity to fail a second time. Now, if a student is not passing the course, we (the school staff) change what we are doing. Failing grades are not an acceptable option. If a student fails, it means that we have failed in some way."

The principal went on to say, "We don't care about the State exam. Don't get me wrong, we want our students to all pass the test, but the test is not the target. We know that our math courses cover the material on the state assessment. So our efforts are on making sure students pass the course and learn the material. Grades are the benchmark. If a student earns a passing grade then he/she will easily pass the State exams."

As the Principal continued to answer the question, I thought to myself, "Did this guy train with Gordon Richiusa?" Maybe our Superintendent of Schools is a black belt and the Principal her student? Change a few words here and there, and both administrators were explaining the basic tenants of the Five Bird System. To quote Gordon, "*The Five Bird System focuses on the student's individual needs, boils almost everything down to its five component parts, emphasizes a simplified teaching method, and makes an impact with the teaching and the techniques by always allowing the individual room to experiment and grow.*"

This is what my local district has been able to implement as part of its culture and practice. Five guiding principals are consistently followed....Meeting individual student needs, teacher responsibility to the student, keep things simple, make learning interesting, and recognize that many paths lead to the same goal…The Five Birds System in a nutshell. When you think about it, it is quite amazing that Gordon articulated how to reform public education in his martial arts teaching, philosophy, and practice years before the current reform efforts.

Notes from Gordon Richusa:

I have been a professional educator for more than 25 years, teaching at the elementary, secondary and community college levels. I spent 20 years working as an educator in the L.A. County Jails, working with the inmates in high school subjects and GED preparation, as well as administering the test and coordinating the curriculum for Hacienda La Puente Adult School. My Master of Arts degree is in English Literature. I have a clear, lifetime teaching credential.

When I say that I have been a professional educator, I know that there are some who are *not* teachers and still believe that they also are educators. These people apparently surmise that if they are engaged in any aspect of the business of running a school, district or supplying a school with supplies, then they too are educators. To say it bluntly, based upon the Five Principles of Everything, this is simply not the case. For the sake of semantic agreement, only those who are on the front lines, actively engaged on a daily basis with students (for example teachers, counselors, librarians, mentors, tutors)—or ARE students themselves, pursuing knowledge or learning something in particular—can call themselves educators. In other words, only the people whose primary goal is education are really educators. On the other hand, every one of the ancillary businesses that I've mentioned above (and, in fact EVERY business venture or pursuit that follows the five principles) can be seen as a valid strategic pursuit that can benefit the individuals who are involved in the various forms, on a five principles scale.

You're not an educator just because you are involved in the business of education; you're not a lifeguard just because you know how to swim; you're not a writer just because you know how to put together a sentence, and you're not a martial artists just because you call yourself master. The difference in all of these examples is a willingness by the individual to take responsibility for their knowledge, skill or position, while maintaining an attention to the Core Human Values found in the Five Principles.

In short, regardless of title, or how closely a person controls education funding or negotiations—cannot be educators unless they have a classroom and curriculum or they are students in a classroom with curriculum.

As usual, "words, their denotation and their connotations" are an important concern for me. Today I'd like to differentiate between two more words: Zen and Tao. Neither one of these things is a religion unto itself, but conjures up religious connotations that sometimes prevent some, with a particular religious belief to close off the benefits of that may be garnered from examination. Taoism is the belief that the Universe runs according to definite rules and principles and that the "why" of a conduct of behavior is more important than the "who, what or when" of it.

Zen, on the other hand, generally defines a particular method for achieving a certain *end (such as enlightenment)*...even though the *end* (or goal) is at times vague and shifting. Zen is usually associated with Buddhism, but is not exclusive to it.

With that, let's examine today's goal. I like to boil everything down to the essential parts, using the Five Principles, as the both the starting point and the ultimate objective. These "essence statements" go by many names. I call them: Concept Training or Capsule Reviews. The capsule of any endeavor is the essential parts of the defining characteristics that summarize what the related principle is and how it relates to what we are trying to accomplish. For instance, the essential concepts of business are probably 1) Supply and Demand and 2) Regardless whether you are in a service business or product business, you still must understand you still must understand the relationship of the market to the customer.

The essential parts of writing, speaking or reading are: 1) Communication is the ultimate goal for each and 2) There are many different ways and purposes to the process of communication.

The essentials of swimming are: 1) Propelling a human body through the water is the ultimate goal and 2) keeping the laws of physics and body mechanics in mind, there are many different reasons why a person might want to swim.

The essential parts of governing are: 1) Making laws to control and regulate human activities for the common good (including physical security) and 2) finding ways to prevent unnecessary interference of a governing body in the lives of the governed.

It is possible to turn any of these into a meditation but to do so, we must be certain that all five principles are being considered, none are being violated. In this way we elevate what we are doing (hopefully engaging one on the levels Mind, Body and Spirit) to a whole new plane. In other words, our thinking about our discipline, our actions related to it and the perspective from which we view this relationship—in the way that being a teacher or being a student, might allow you to become a TRUE educator—can alter the most mundane into the sublime. Anything can become a meditation.

In my classrooms, I give this information to students on the first day so that they can begin to understand where I am coming from. I tell them that my class is one of the best that they will ever take because, regardless of their particular point of reference, I am dedicated to helping them succeed within the confines of the course objectives to apply what I can teach to their own specific perspective. In other words, I think there are certain "ways" that will be beneficial from which they can concentrate on learning English, and my goal is to find out how to make their goals work in harmony.

To achieve my goal, I take very specific direction from all my former teachers (especially those in the martial arts) who were successful in accomplishing both THEIR goals and my own. Naturally, there were times in the learning process that I did not hold up my part of the bargain. The "good or great" teachers did not sway from their particular course objectives in these cases. They merely found new and inventive ways to say the same things that they were saying to the rest of the class. Indeed, sometimes it took me years (even decades) to grasp a particular lesson fully, or in some cases to even benefit slightly from a lesson.

Life and Death Objective

By John Gates, U.S. Army, Retired

My name is John Gates. I have known Gordon for nearly 30 years. When I met Gordon, I was a young teen martial arts student, he was a visiting guest instructor, and we instantly clicked. Gordon, in many ways, was a big influence on me becoming a man. Besides being the consummate martial arts instructor, tailoring my instruction to my needs and personality, he has also been a really good friend.

I have a lot of stories about Gordon, but I think this one shows his adherence to the Five Principles. I was 18 years old; I had dropped out of high school a couple of years previously for many different reasons. I wasn't living at home and spent a good deal of time living with Gordon and his family. At this time Gordon was an Adult Educator in the LA County jail system, primarily working north of Los

Angeles at the Pitchess Ranch Facility. Gordon knew my story, knew who I was and who I could be. He also knew what a great obstacle being a high school dropout could be.

He worked kind of strange shifts, going into work and coming home at rather odd hours during the day. One late afternoon, as I was eating yet another meal at his house, he told me to go get dressed and make sure I wear a button down shirt. At the time I didn't have any with me and had to borrow one. I kept asking him what he had planned, but knowing Gordon, I knew just to go with the flow and it would all work out. As one of Gordon's martial arts students I knew training often took on a spontaneous nature. We were always going on what he called, *Adventures*. He told me that he was going to take me to work with him and that I was going to take my GED that night. I had done enough research to know what a GED was and that it could "replace" my missing high school diploma, but I hadn't studied at all for it.

That night, he sat me in one of the back offices after parading me past the inmates to make an impression on me. He administered my GED while he worked with the inmates in the main classroom. A few weeks later my certificate arrived. Without any preparation at all, I had passed. I felt a whole world had opened up; I was a "success" again. I have gone on to a very successful 22-year career with the United

States Army in the Communications field. I'm just two classes short of completing the requirements for my Bachelor's Degree. Not too bad for a high school dropout.

The Five Principles as I understand them are as follows:

Awareness - Being aware of not only your surroundings; the place you are, the people around you, the objects, but also being aware of YOURSELF.

Flow - This principle covers not only movement, but also economy of movement. It's about knowing when to "Sprint" and when to jog. It's also about finding the unobstructed way around the obstacle instead of bull dozing through it.

Form - This principle is about HOW you act. It can cover how you dress to meet the world, how you interact with the world, or how you perform your act.

Benefit - Literally, "What's in it for me?" but also identifying whatever benefit you decide as a goal. Keep your eye on the prize.

Harmony - Being in Harmony is easier said than done. In your OWN world, it should be relatively simple; but, in a foreign environment, it could take a lot of work. Part of this is to be in Harmony with YOURSELF, never compromising who you are or what you believe in.

Gordon followed all five of the principles when he took me to take my GED. How have the Five Principles worked in my life as a Professional Soldier? Well, let's take a look at that.

As a soldier during day to day activities, I had to stay **Aware** of not only my surroundings but also of myself, what my short, mid, and long term goals were that I had set for myself. Being aware of not only my leaders and my peers, but most importantly of my subordinates, of the example I was setting. As they say, "young eyes are always watching" and this is no truer than with young soldiers. Mentoring young men and women is a tough enough job, but it's tougher when they are able to watch your every move and act. Setting the example for them, as a Non-Commissioned Officer, is a full time job, in and out of uniform.

Being aware is also important in combat. The potential threats and enemy, your actual job, the allies around you, these are all things you have to keep in consideration while making a plan of action. Taking into account your subordinates, how they perform, how they are feeling, who is good at what; again, all things that are important to keep in mind. The best plan of action on paper can be ruined in the first 5 minutes of implementation because the leader failed to take into account his soldiers.

It is also important to remain conscious *during* a task. Seeing an obstruction before it's too late to change the game can be just as important to accomplishing your goal as choosing your goal to begin with. “Hitting the wall” in full stride not only interrupts progress, but also can be demoralizing and affect everyone around you in a negative way. Seeing the course around the obstacle in time to take advantage not only keeps “the ball rolling”, but also keeps spirits high as everyone sees the progress being made.

I had to stay in the **Flow**, knowing when to run hard and knowing when to remember economy of motion. I had to know what the intent of my commanders above me was, and how to accomplish my mission within those guidelines. Doing my best job, getting the best out of my soldiers, meant absolutely nothing, if what I was doing wasn’t supporting my commander’s vision.

As a leader I always had to remember what we were doing, why we were doing it, and when it needed to be done by. The 90% solution, on time or early, is always better than the 100% solution late. I had to keep an eye on my soldiers, ensuring that they didn’t burn themselves out. I also had to make sure that they carried their fair share of weight and someone else wasn’t burning out picking up their slack. This was also important for me to remember, as it did no good to provide unbridled leadership for 3 weeks and be utterly useless for the rest of a 9-month deployment because I had made myself sick.

I had to remember **Form** at all times, from taking care of my appearance and uniform to how I performed my job. The way you accomplish a task can be almost as important as what you accomplish. The idea that, "*if it isn't pretty, but it works*" can sometimes be true. However, in life, the journey is just as important as the destination. I could be the best super soldier the Army has ever seen; but if I get that way by climbing the backs of other soldiers to do it, or by lying, or by any number of other things that compromise the journey, then the accomplishment itself doesn't really mean much.

Form involves the idea that if it's important enough to do, then it's important enough to do RIGHT. The concept is that you consciously choose the actions that you take, and then you perform those actions to the upmost of your ability. Most people go through day-to-day tasks half asleep, unconscious about what they are doing. When they look back they wonder where the day went and why so many things that they do look or feel half finished. The idea is that you remain present at all times, thinking and experiencing what you are doing at all times.

Benefit in the Army is a hard one. On one hand, there are the personal goals that you set for yourself; education, travel, and even finances: but the Army is built on mission accomplishment and the good of the greater purpose. The balance between those two ideals can make life interesting at times for soldiers. Maintaining that balance is important, as it does no good for the person to have a great military career and have no personal goals met; it also does no good for a military career to have all your personal goals met by neglecting the Army's big picture.

People in life do things for one of three main reasons; Financial Success, Professional Success, or Personal Success. Financial success is one of the easiest to define and one of the hardest to pinpoint. As so many people have said lately, "How much money is enough money?" You do it for the money, easy enough to understand, you are willing to do whatever it takes, work the hours, suffer the indignities to get you where you want to go. Soldiers, for the most part, don't join the Army to get rich.

Professional success is also pretty easy to define. Getting that promotion, working your way up the company ladder, being the "go to" person at your company which supervisors, peers, and subordinates alike admire. The stumbling block comes in when you climb that ladder at all costs, stepping on the backs of your peers and subordinates to do it. The good part about the Army is that professional success is rather easy to identify; earning a promotion, earning an award, being recognized in front of your unit by commanders, all things that readily give you feedback that you are a success. When you finally leave the Army, and the only thing to show for it is a shadow box with your awards and decorations— you have no hobbies, no education, a family in disrepair, and feel absolutely lost— is that really a "success"?

Personal success is the much more difficult to define idea. It's difficult in that it's about what makes YOU happy. The old adage, "if you aren't having fun anymore, then you shouldn't be doing it," fits in here. Personal success could be defined as "You work to LIVE" rather than you LIVE to work, or you go to work to support your hobbies. Your success could be defined by not what you do on the job, but what you do OFF the job, in that your job allows you the ability to do what it is that you want to do. Personal success could also be defined on the job. Mentoring young Soldiers comes to mind as a Personal accomplishment. Personally improving in your career field (being technically competent) could be another. As you see, it really could be anything that makes YOU happy, either in or out of work.

The key about a benefit, a goal as it were, is to identify it from the get go. You could establish short, mid, and long-term goals (as is done in martial arts with the *kyu* system: belts and dans), to take the journey in shorter bite-sized chunks. Identifying the Benefit for the "Group" is also important, as they understand what they are setting out to accomplish and it is easier to keep them motivated toward that goal. Setting realistic goals is also important, as if you put things too far out of reach, then it becomes almost demoralizing to work toward.

Living in **Harmony** seems almost like a foreign concept when discussing the Army. The Army's overall single most important mission is "To Search for, Close with, and Destroy the enemy"; not very harmonious in its reading. The idea of trying to move 500,000 soldiers toward that single purpose without Harmony would be an impossible task; all the soldiers have to be working toward that single purpose with intent.

I've talked earlier about setting the example for Soldiers/subordinates. Living in personal Harmony or balance is a good way to "set the example". Think of it as the parent that tells their child not to smoke as they are puffing away on a Marlboro. Telling your soldiers that they need to have balance, to work, play, learn, live, love, worship, and all the great things that life has to offer, if you don't personally set the example yourself, is contradictory.

Remember, there is Always balance in the Universe. Light/Dark, Good/Evil, Hot/Cold, for every action, there is an equal and opposite Reaction. Living in harmony could also mean to not live in any ONE extreme. The Chinese Ying/Yang symbol is a perfect example. It represents not only Light and Dark, but more importantly, Male and Female. In the symbol, they are in balance, neither one having more weight than the other. Goju Ryu Martial Arts is another example, Go is Hard and Ju is Soft, literally the Martial Art takes the Hard lines of the Japanese and the Soft Circles of the Chinese and incorporates them together in balance.

So, as you can see, while it's not an easy task to live as a Modern Soldier while following the Five Principles; not only can it be done, but it almost HAS to be done whether consciously or not. The same holds true in life. Awareness, Flow, Form, Benefit and Harmony have a place in not only every occupation, but everyone's life as a whole. The Principles are guides as are Parents, Codes, Laws, and even Religions. As guides, and not "dogmatic", they lend themselves to assist people in life's endeavors and not stifle or hamstring the individual, that's the Harmonious part.

(John Gates is a lifelong Martial Artist with a black belt in The Five Birds System, a recreational drummer, a retired Soldier having achieved the rank of Sergeant First Class, and more. Constantly striving to learn and grow as a man, he currently lives outside of Chambersburg, Pennsylvania with his beautiful wife Lisa. What life has in store for will be is anyone's guess, but it's going to be good.)

The Way of Archery

(NOTE: Gordon Richiusa has published the following article many times, in many forms. Here is the first compilation of these articles with Five Principle applications. This and other abstracts are submitted here, NOT merely as a addendum to the specific topic of teaching archery, or martial arts, but as an example of what this particular subject and the way that it is taught can teach us about the process of teaching and learning in general. It is felt that shooting an arrow toward an obvious bull's eye is a universally accepted metaphor that cannot be ignored.)

It seems like I've always been an archer. I can remember, at a young age building bows with my brother. I competed in high school on the archery team and carried my arrows and bows with me throughout the world. In 1980 I had the pleasure of moving to Oahu, Hawaii to live, work and learn. One of the experiences that I had was to study Kyudo (traditional Japanese Zen Archery) with a group who gathered at the base of Diamond Head on a weekly basis to practice this unique form of Zen Meditation. Masters would come from Japan on a monthly basis to demonstrate technique and to encourage a devotion to purity.

Simply stated, in Kyudo the archer, the bow the arrow, the target and the process all become one with the ultimate goal of awareness of our spiritual selves.

Without belaboring the subject, it is necessary to say that Zen Archery is heavily laden with the study and practice of Buddhism and so the shot is divided into eight parts symbolizing the eightfold path of enlightenment. I am not a Buddhist, but when I returned to Los Angeles (after a stay in Idaho) I continued to practice and to study with a Master Mishima of a Los Angeles Buddhist Temple. I also was in the process (as was my nature) of developing a kind of Archery Meditation that incorporated other teachings from which I had benefited.

I had the experience of working and learning from a number of Native Americans, in a variety of ways, including martial arts training. The subject of archery often came up.

Their style of constructing and shooting a bow was very different from the Japanese Zen Master, although there was one important similarity. The experience of shooting an arrow was a very spiritual one. In both the American and the Japanese styles of shooting, the bow when fully drawn creates a circle. The circle or hoop are sacred symbols of the spiritual path in both, diverse cultures.

When I began to incorporate archery into my teaching of martial arts, I was given a Flemish Long Bow by one of my students, which cannot physically be held or shot in exactly the same way as the other two methods that I'd studied. I had also begun to attempt the transformation of all my thinking into the Five Birds method. Today, therefore I have divided the shot into—you guessed it—five parts.

The ultimate goals of the shot are the same as those learned through practice of the eastern and western styles of shooting. The only differences are that my method can be used with ANY bow, any arrow, any target, any skill level and any archer. The act of shooting an arrow is largely symbolic and ritualistic. The stance one takes, the number of parts the shot is divided into and even the number of breaths that one takes (or how one breathes) all have greater meaning for all styles of shooting, otherwise one is not doing anything more than launching a small spear toward a target. I have divided the conversation about archery into five parts, as usual.

Many people get tense at the sound of the word "meditation," simply because they have given over to it too much significance. I have even heard some people say that it is "dangerous" to meditate unless you are contemplating some particular facet of their chosen religion. The word "evil" is sometimes tossed about in relationship to what some people consider "other" or "not sanctioned" forms of meditation.

All this stress and worry is extremely counterproductive. No wonder people have such a conflict in their first meditation classes when the teacher utters the phrase, "O.K. now just relax." There is simply no point of reference for such a thing!

To me, meditation is merely a state of mind, body and spirit usually referred to as a "heightened, relaxed or completely clear" state of being where the overall being can function at its most beneficial level. This would not, therefore allow for any "dangerous" condition to exist. There is no possibility of evil. That is the position that we start from in this book.

In the arena of psychology it is also generally accepted that human beings learn in three basic ways. They are: Auditory, Visually and Tactually. This means that we learn by what we are told or what we hear. Or we learn by what we are shown or what we see. Or we learn by what we do or what we feel. Some people favor one mode of learning over another, which is why education classes guide teachers to teach to all of the strengths of their students. For instance, if a teacher just writes something on the board and haves a student read it they are teaching on one modality level. If they say the words that the students are reading (as in lecture with a blackboard) they are teaching on two levels. If they have the students copy the words in their own notes that they are seeing and hearing, then we are working at all three levels.

Generally, in the world of meditation it is accepted that there are two kinds of meditation, active and passive or moving and seated meditation. Within these two ends of the same spectrum there are variations which try to combine aspects of each (such as yoga) or rely more heavily on one of the five senses or another (as with the use of chanting, drums, bells, sand-painting or other finger or body positions or even oils, incense or other fragrances) offering an experience on more than one level. Actually, in meditation the kind of meditation is divided into three distinct types, "Mudra (hand and body positions), Midra (sounds and smells) and Mandela (pictures)."

My intent is not to apply any undue value to one form of meditation over another or to pursue an argument that one form of meditation is better than another. This article is merely to explain the origins of Archery as Meditation in the Five Birds System of Martial Arts and to offer direction to those who which to pursue this wonderful art. It is my hope that every person who loves to draw an arrow, or even to witness others in this pursuit, will gain something from this writing. I teach Archery as Meditation, because it is one of the "ways" that I learned to meditate, to benefit on a number of levels, to gain health, happiness and a sense of completeness. For these reasons, I thank my teachers for not ever limiting me to any particular form of meditation as the only path to enlightenment. In addition, I would like to express my gratitude to my students (especially the young ones) who have helped me to broaden and refine my thinking and teaching techniques over the years.

A History and Explanation of Japanese Zen Archery

If asked which of the many forms of traditional martial arts is the deadliest, the answers would be as numerous as the styles there are to study. Qualify this question, however, to include only those arts which are effective up to 100 yards from an opponent, and the field of answers would be narrowed to only one.

Zen archery or KYUDO (meaning, "the way of the bow") is a martial art that literally stands alone among all fighting arts. It is a martial art that is really a Japanese form of Zen meditation, and has no violence and no opponents. Ideally, training in any martial art should contain some sort of work by an individual alone (including weapons such as katana or bo) in the form of kata. But, it is the Zen archer alone who must always pit himself against himself to become part of the process of understanding that is hitting a target with an arrow.

The goals in Zen archery are characteristic of all Zen teachings. They are as elusive as trying to catch the wind in your hands. For, in the end, the archer can truly have no goals; in the end, the awareness or concept of archery, the target, the bow, the arrow and the archer must become one thing.

The beauty of this form of martial arts movement and its value to all others lay in its ability to expand the precepts of the fighting arts for the viewer onto a grand scale, while at the same time restricting the motions to a concise series of repeated, ritualized and meaning-filled movements.

All Zen archers perform the movements in the exact same methodical way. Master and student learn to flow with the same energy and therefore reap the same benefits. The ultimate result of hitting the bull's eye is an immediate one that even the uneducated viewer knows the value of. If the archer does not perform the motions correctly, totally relaxed and without personal concern for hitting his goal, the arrow will simply not find its mark. A mistake is that obvious.

On the other hand, if one should happen to accidentally hit the bull's eye and know in his heart that the movements were not performed in the proper spirit of concentration, then this too is of no value. There is no one to try to fool. For, shooting the arrow without the proper spirit is something else; it is not true Zen. What sets the master apart from the student is that he can both hit the bull's eye with great regularity and at the same time, not care that he is doing so.

As I said, there are eight precise stages of shooting an arrow in this fashion. Each stage is roughly associated with the eightfold path of Buddhist philosophy. It must be remembered that all of the stages are performed with an unusual attention to exactness, while at the same time; the archer must be totally relaxed. There is a practical reason for this, beyond the religious significance. If the archer, for instance is not relaxed from the initial stages of the shot and remains so throughout his tension can cause a number of painful results. In kyudo there is a saying, "The bow is a good teacher." For another curious attribute of the kyudo form is that the bow must be allowed to spin freely after the shot. No forearm guard is worn. The string actually spins entirely around the hand, from one side of the arm to the other. If this is not allowed to take place, there is another Zen archery expression that applies, "The bow will punish you." The string will slap the archer's arm. It is a lesson that need be experienced but once to be learned. On the other hand, as a final tribute to the Zen method, the archer always holds a second arrow in the little finger of the string hand, reminding him that ultimately, the last shot, regardless where it falls on the target will always be replaced by the next arrow.

Those who embrace the art of kyudo as their way to enlightenment must be prepared for years of training. There are two diverse training methods, which meet at the form that is described here. The first (and most traditional) is to teach a student to breathe properly and relax, and perhaps even perform the motions of shooting for up to a year and a half before he is allowed to actually shoot his first arrow. Moreover, the practitioner must ritualistically prepare all of his own equipment by hand. That is precisely what the traditional archer is taught to do by his sensei (teacher).

Arrows are sanded smooth from a special type of strong, thin bamboo. Hawk or eagle feathers are cut to shape and glued into place. The arrow nocking point is meticulously wound around with string and tied by hand. Every detail of preparation is performed as the act of shooting the arrow. Even stringing the bow or walking onto the field are considered part of the process and are performed with reverence.

The other method is to give an arrow and bow to the student and tell them to shoot a set number of arrows (sometimes 1000) daily. No formal instruction will take place for up to one and a half years. During this initial stage the student irons out most of the specifics on his or her own and then the teacher merely refines the process.

I was instructed with a little of both ends of the spectrum. Master Mishima contended that every student was unique and the master was like a person sitting on top of a mountain instructing many people, coming from many different directions, with various obstacles in front of him or her on the best way to get to where he was. "Sometime a person may not see that if they go straight ahead they will fall into a great hole. Another must be told to turn left or right to avoid other obstacles. They do not have the advantage of looking down on the situation to see what the best path is." In other words, one student should not concern himself with what the teacher is telling another student. If a student who “should go straight” follows the directions given to another to “turn left” there could be dire result!

Whatever route one pursues, it will generally take years before the student can master the basic elements of kyudo. There are then ten levels of mastery that may be reached by the archer. It is no wonder that the art is often considered the archer's best friend after so long a personal relationship with the process. When asked why he continued to shoot his bow everyday, in any weather, without fail, on Kyudo master replied, “ Even if I no longer had a bow or the strength to pull the arrow back, I would continue to perform the motions in midair and empty handed. I have learned the most valuable lesson from kyudo. I am no longer an archer who shoots his arrows with a bow. I am a part of the process.”

The Five Stages of the Five Birds Archery Shot

The question, at this point should naturally arise, “Why Five?” As I have already said, the Zen archer divides his shot into eight stages to align himself with the eightfold path of Buddha.

I am not a Buddhist and have learned, at the same time to appreciate the value of pursuing spiritual mediation through archery while knowing that, as Mishima might have put it,

“There are many kinds of mountains to climb.” In other words, I don't believe that a person must pursue Buddhism (you can insert any other name of a religion, discipline or focus here) to gain value from archery as a “way” to enlightenment, or as an enhancement to the perspective that one is pursuing.

For me, the number five works. It coincides with my own personal belief system and it's easy for me to teach it to those who are interested in my style of martial arts.

Having said that, I have divided the shot into five parts in this manner:

1) Preparing to shoot
2) Focus on the goal
3) Lifting the bow
4) Draw and release
5) Savoring the shot

There are, of course several layers or aspects of each of these stages, and, plenty of room for individual creativity. For instance, when one “prepares to shoot” they are putting themselves not only in the proper mood and attitude, but also in the appropriate stance with the proper equipment. Again, there are variations. I was taught (and sometimes teach) that the archer does not even need a bow, arrow or target to perform the shot. Indeed, I must say that even when I was physically unable to raise or draw a bow, I still performed the task in my mind and heart on a daily basis.

For most purposes, however I recommend that archery can be performed with any bow, at any draw poundage at any distance using any of a number of "anchor points."

I prefer a Flemish Long Bow, about 65 lbs. of pull (these days), but I have used a recurve and even own a compound. Now that I think of it, I have even used a blowgun following a similar ritual and gotten adequate results.

I don't recommend any mechanically enhanced bows (compound, assisted draw or cross bow) simply because I have yet to be able to figure out how to make the fluidity of the shot work with these devices. This is not to say that it can't be done. I merely say that I have not done it, and I really have no intention of putting the time into it to change my habits now. The shot I use suits me and is sufficient to the end, which is to transcend the shot and relax into a state of heightened awareness.

The preceding abstract article can be accessed through the blog (www.5birdsmartialarts.blogspot.com) or at the communication website (www.vision-revision.pbwiki.com). Both are free. However, it is requested that you subscribe at these sites, if you are utilizing them. Thanks.

The Gradual Diet

By Barbara Rich (AKA Ageless1der)

Words like cold turkey, shock to your system, drastic change or sudden cut back all tends to scare people away from making changes in their diets. I have never been a believer in the "no pain no gain" concept. For that reason, I recommend that you take it nice and easy. Sound good?

One steady drop of water, over a period of time will get the same results as a sudden flood. That single drop, continuously applied will erode the most stubborn rock. The most difficult part about dieting is getting started. So let's start easy. The method I have developed is called "The Gradual Diet," and it is for those who are clearly in need of losing some weight but have a tough time with the whole concept of dieting. The keys are: knowing yourself, knowing how much weight you truly need to lose, and the point at which a diet becomes a lifestyle change.

Here's how it works:

Begin by cutting in half what you would eat on a normal day. It doesn't matter what you ordinarily eat, the kind of food or the amount. Only know that you are going to cut that amount in half. Don't worry; you will not starve. Your body will feel comforted by the fact that it is familiar with the kind of food that it is getting. You may feel a little bit hungry, but that's o.k. It is best to get a realistic idea of the amount of food you are ordinarily eating before you begin. Many times people will sabotage their good choices by suddenly increasing the amount of food intake, before they begin a diet. This is panic eating and panic dieting. What I recommend is kind of like sneaking up on your self. So just allow yourself the opportunity to cut back. On the other hand every individual has specific dietary needs and nutritional requirements. What I am recommending here is for those who are definitely overweight and have tried other diets and failed.

So, after you've cut in half a single day's worth of eating, the next day go back to your old diet. This doesn't mean that you are now overeating, just eating what is normal for you.

Relax and be comfortable with the process. Repeat this pattern for a week. One day you follow the new or gradual diet; the next day you follow the old diet. The second week, add a gradual diet day. Cut in half your old diet for two days and then go back to a regular course of meals for one. Do this for two weeks. After two weeks, increase your diet days to three. Do this for three weeks and so on.

Notice that to get to a place where you are "dieting" more than you are following old patterns will take a month and a half. Clearly, you will not see as drastic a change as you might have with other diets because you are not starving yourself. You are changing your habits gradually. However, you will definitely be eating fewer calories, therefore you WILL SEE POSITIVE RESULTS. Remember, I am using the arbitrary amount of half, based on the assumption that you are overweight from eating too much. The object is to think in terms of getting what you need to be healthy, rather than what you have become used to consuming.

Further Options

You are going to love this part. You actually get to choose your diet food. On your diet day, if you do not want to do half portions you can choose the Zone, Weight Watchers, South Beach, etc. It really doesn't matter which program's meals you prefer. You can even alternate your diet choices on your diet days. The bottom line is: it is all about calories. This method gradually changes your lifestyle of eating. You will always have one day a week when you can satisfy your cravings. Go a little crazy, but always return to your moderate eating. We all have special occasions, such as weddings, showers or birthdays and we shouldn't have to give up everything associated with celebrating. Work around these special occasions. Allow yourself to enjoy the food you eat on these days. You can do it!

Exercise

Exercise on the gradual program is viewed in the same way that eating is. Start easy and work yourself up to more exercise days. You get to choose if you want to exercise on the old diet or new diet day. Like the diet, find a pace and a style of exercise that works well for you at first and gradually increase your exercise program. Naturally, if you are starting with zero exercise then an increase will be simple. Remember, ANY amount of exercise is better than none.

I suggest starting with simple walking. As you start losing weight you will feel better and be able to walk further and faster and even to try other, more advanced exercise. If your health permits more strenuous exercise, then by all means do so. Remember it's all about calories-the number of your intake versus the amount you burn. I prefer moderation to extremes. I believe in being good to my body and it will be good to me. I don't push it beyond its limits. I might also mention I don't like pain. You don't have to suffer terrible consequences to get fit. You do have to be dedicated to a lifestyle that keeps you happy and healthy. You can get lazy about dieting if your attitude is that of defeat.

Attitude is Everything

Another very important aspect of this diet is attitude. Attitude is another choice. See, you are in control of your attitude, so pick a good one. Right? I get a visual picture of myself at my best and make that a goal. If your imagination is not that vivid, then find a picture of yourself that pleases you and place it on your refrigerator or anywhere you can see it as a constant reminder of what you will achieve.

Keep a calendar of "old diet/ new diet days." It will motivate you to stay with it.

Your exercise program should also be recorded. Once you have programmed yourself to this lifestyle it won't be necessary to keep records, it will become a part of you.

Educate Yourself

I can remember how shocked I was when I read on a cereal box (nutritional) that it is 130 calories for a single serving. I noticed that the serving was 1/2 cup, so for some reason I decided to take out a measuring cup and see how much cereal that really was. I measured a 1/2 cup of cereal. It is not much. It certainly was not a full bowl of cereal. I started to measure everything that I was eating and I was amazed! The recommended serving sizes were ALWAYS smaller than the amounts I was used to consuming.

What's the conclusion? Keep a measuring cup on hand. If we look at that bowl of cereal once again, when you add milk it increases to 180 calories. So beware of the amount of food that is equal to a serving. Sometime you think, well I only had a bowl of cereal and WOW! it could be close to 400 calories if you have eaten it with a full cup of milk. Read the labels carefully and compare. It may be worth it to you to get a little bit more food or eat something that tastes better but may have a few more calories. Either way, your decisions will be based on facts.

Desserts and Rewards

Positive reinforcement is better than punishment. So, I say reward *yourself*! One of my favorite meals is dessert. I don't think I'm alone in this. Most people like dessert more than anything else. One of my favorite desserts on my diet days is a delicious good-sized fudgecicle with only 100 calories. There are quite a few out there. I like "Skinny

Cow." They are tasty and satisfying. I use substitute sugars whenever possible, or no sweetener at all. Splenda, Equal etc., anything that doesn't have any calorie content is always going to be a better choice in the long run. Use these substitutes on oatmeal, fruit, anywhere you would ordinarily use sugar. It really makes a difference. Don't forget herbs. There are no calories in a sprinkling of herbs. A little olive oil and rice vinegar complimented with oregano, sweet basil or dill adds a distinctive flavor. Everyone has a favorite herb. Pick yours and enjoy! A lot of the nutrition bars are high in calories, originally meant to build the body with proteins. Some of these health bars are substitutes for meals, not snacks. What that means is if you have a bar for lunch, then that is your lunch. Most of these bars need to be cut in half for a snack. There are some bars that are only 120 calories, but they are small.

Yogurt is another good choice at snack time. Shop around. Read the labels. You may find that you will be better able to stick to the good stuff the more educated you become about your body. Yogurt is especially healthy for women because of the calcium content. Raw veggies are healthy, but did you know the dressing you dip them into is high in calories? I mix olive oil and seasoned rice vinegar in a jar and keep it to dip my veggies. I use it on my salads and also as a marinade for chicken. It's the little dips and dollops that increase your fat intake. Thank goodness for lite whipped topping. Two tablespoons are only 28 calories. Top your cakes and desserts with whipped topping instead of icing or real whipped cream. When applying dressings such as your favorite brand of mayonnaise or mustard, read the label to determine what a "rational amount" might be. Drink diet soft drinks instead of sugar filled ones. Better yet, try tea as a substitute for soda or coffee. Did you know that oolong and green tea actually boost your metabolism? Try hot tea in cool weather, iced tea in the warmer weather. You will gradually acquire a taste for these substitutes and include them in your lifestyle.

Don't get discouraged. Your weight will fluctuate. Give it 6 to 8 weeks. The more overweight you are the quicker you will see a weight loss. The less weight you have to lose, the longer it will take because your maintenance is at a lower calorie intake. Your body has taken time to adjust its metabolism to maintain your present weight. It will take time to reset itself.

The Miracle Body

Your body is a healing machine. This magnificent machine compares to no other. The inner workings of the body are just astounding. The filtering and purifying of antibodies, the distribution of nutrients to various organs in the body is just a few of the myriad of functions the body deals with on a daily basis. We know that the care we give a treasured machine will insure its performance and endurance. Let's treat our body in the same way and with the same respect we treat any other machine in our lives. Do not abuse or, don't laugh, torture it. Yes, overloaded and sluggish bodies resort to reserve status, which forces the body to be laboring constantly and exhausting all its resources. Love your body and demonstrate this love through action and your body will love you.

Don't Beat Yourself Up

Be kind and good to yourself. Some days will be harder than others. It's O.K. Keep moving forward. Pick yourself up and start all over again. Even a bad day has the promise of a better tomorrow. Don't lose sight of your goal. This life plan is not designed to promote self-destructive behavior. It's not a matter of being a Pollyanna or wearing rose colored glasses, ignoring your faults. It's a matter of emphasizing the positive and keeping sight of your goals.

Ah, Youth! (And health)

Youth so fleeting...how do we hold onto this dream? The physical aspect of youth has been denied those of maturity.

However, the heart and spirit can remain young forever. The choice is ours.

When our hearts and spirits are young it brings out a youthful countenance. So, why not begin within? Change your attitude to one of vitality, regardless of your limitations. Be as vital as physically possible.

Start a Youth List. This could be something as formal as a journal or an unconnected as scribbled post-its on the side of your fridge. It is always a good idea to have something to refer to keep you on track. A Youth List is a way to remind yourself of a good idea you may want to experiment with or a tried and true method you've found to feel and stay young. The U.S. Army says, "Be the best that you can be."

Seniors (and I make this special plea to seniors, since I am one of them), we can start out by eating better and exercising. Once we are at our physical potential, we can become a part of the exciting things around us. Travel shows, social gatherings, these things practically propel us to feeling young. Surrounded by life and its offerings keeps us motivated. Stop and think about what I am saying. Think of all the things we CAN do. It actually forces us into life. And here's the kicker, we are wiser now and skip the pitfalls that youth must endure. I hope you are patting yourself on the back. Rejoice! You have reached the age of maturity with enthusiasm and wisdom! Look at yourself, your reading a book about meeting your full potential!

Now, let's concentrate on the aspects of optimum health so that we can benefit with optimum potential in all other aspects of our lives! Let's look at Diet as all the things that we do to keep our bodies in optimum health, concentrating (not obsessing) on every aspect of our plan to ensure that we are gaining the maximum benefits from our chosen strategy. In this way, Diet can become our form of meditation.

As the Taoists may put it, "Observing yourself through the eye of the Perfect Observer, you may become your perfect self."

Desires, Wishes, Prayers and Strategies

There is a vast difference between desires, wishes, prayers and plans. They all represent various levels of the same thing, an application of our awareness.

When I was sixteen years old—on my birthday—a very important event occurred in my life. I became self aware and especially aware of the aging process. The moment is as vivid in my mind now, as it was more than fifty years ago. I realized that I could never be sixteen again! Sitting alone on my bed, I realized I could never go back in time. It wasn't that I had a particularly perfect childhood. I wasn't one of the "popular" girls or one of the "in crowd" or "rich kids." I just knew that life was a unique and special experience, regardless of what it had in store for me. I also realized that youth is one of life's greatest gifts. I was concerned (strike that—I was suddenly terrified) that growing old the way that I'd seen others do it, would limit my ability to live life to the fullest. Isn't that an odd worry for someone who just turned sixteen? I did not know, at the time (1952) that we could appreciate life from a complex number of perspectives.

I decided to pray for youth. My desire was innocent and sincere beyond anything I'd ever hoped for in my short existence. I prayed and wept. My mother heard my crying and did not know how to console me. She was not one for solving her own or other's problems, a very shy and reserved woman. But then, my dad came home.

"You are just a kid," he smiled and soothed me with his words. "You have so much of life ahead of you. Every year a new adventure awaits you."

My father lived to his 90th year. Even when we were both of much more advanced age then when he first gave me the advice, he still said the same thing to me: *You're just a kid.*

I can never be sixteen again, but I can return to any year with the memories I have woven from each adventure.

My advice here (like everything else) is simple. Make the most of every age. Be the best you can be *at the time*. If you follow this advice, your Book Of Life will be witness to others that prayers are answered.

Happiness is fleeting, but still a valid pursuit

"Are you happy?"

When people ask me that question I have a hard time answering it. Happiness is not a condition. Taking this viewpoint, we see that we may have happy times, but things and times change. The ability to adapt to these changes in a positive way is the key. As a child I struggled with disappointment. If I was told I couldn't go to the beach because of the weather or the car broke down, I pouted and was miserable all day. What a waste!

Life will surprise you. Don't think of every surprise as a mere disappointment. Put a positive spin on it. Movies are great on rainy days. Have a friend over for lunch and a chat. We all love to talk and listen about all the neighborhood scuttlebutt. The point I'm making is, "Adapt and wait. Something will happen." Understand the difference between resisting and not giving up.

Hold onto your dreams, but go with the flow of life. Be open to what might be best for you. If you can be content (not in a rut) where you are in life and accept things for that time, doors will open to many possibilities that when chosen push you to another level. We can all have our share of happiness if we choose to. A door will only open when you let go of circumstances and situations that "lock you up." Pursuing Happiness is much easier when you have a clear picture of what that means TO YOU.

Think of your Diet as a form of Meditation

You can turn your meals into a spiritual act. Many cultures pray at mealtimes. I think this is a great idea for those who believe in prayer. Some people believe that every action is a prayer and that eating is just another action. I see a great wisdom in this way of thinking. You can easily turn your diet into a form of meditation, especially if you include the preparation and the choices we make in the kinds of foods that we eat.

A Right and Wrong Solution

The difference between "weight loss programs" and "healthy diets" is the difference between success and failure, in my opinion. Every life strategy should include a fair evaluation of the pitfalls of the plan, such as Diet Obsessive behavior (bulimia or anorexia, for instance). Use common sense. If something is hurting you more than it is helping, then stop doing it! Remember the old joke of a guy walking into a doctor and saying, "Doc, it hurts when I do this." And, the doctor replies, "Don't do that."

If you are weak, feel pain or have other symptoms that indicate a problem then, for goodness sake see a doctor! In fact, it wouldn't hurt to see a doctor before proceeding with any major change in your lifestyle, eating habits or exercise regimen.

The Bigger the Target, the Easier it is to Hit

Allow your Target Weight to have more than one ring in the *bull's eye*. In other words, allow yourself a wide range of success. If you see that you are moving in the right direction "overall" that in itself is success. Your body weight will naturally fluctuate. You weigh more in the evening than you do in the morning. Some days you drink and retain more water than other days. Your body even changes with the seasons. We are talking about SMALL fluctuations here, not dramatic weight gains. If you weigh 20 pounds more today than you did two weeks ago, that is not normal.

You Are Unique

Everyone is different. That means that each individual has varying needs, as well as different starting points to the same goal. Differences are as obvious as Men vs. Women, Short vs. Tall, and Athletic vs. Sedentary. Sometimes the differences are not so obvious, like hereditary metabolism and cholesterol manufacturing rates.

Differences in age, sex and body type are never more important to consider than with the addition of an exercise program. You've heard it said that there are different strokes for different folks.

I've already told you what I like and what I do. I also told you that my husband is much more athletically inclined than I. He drinks more water, eats more food, can consume more carbohydrates than I can. However, his genetic background also allows his body to produce higher levels of "bad" cholesterol than I do, even when his diet is guarded. Recently, however (after being prescribed cholesterol lowering drugs) he had a heart scan, to measure the amount of blockage that he'd find in his arteries. Low and behold! The percentage of blockage was ZERO in all arteries. He decided that he didn't need to lower his cholesterol. My make-up is faster paced than my husband's. I call myself a sprinter and he, definitely is a long distance person. His metabolism adjusts for changes in diet and exercise making him slower to lose or to gain weight than I, but no one would call either one of us unhealthy.

We have another friend who loves fast food burgers but having his cholesterol checked regularly he never has a problem with an elevated level. He also loves to play tennis, once or twice a week but he does nothing else of a physical nature. Tennis or other sports never interested me, although I love to dance. There are times when I will still put on some old songs and dance around the house while I'm cleaning, or just for the fun of it. The point is this: Unless you are injured or have some other diagnosed infirmity, exercise can't hurt you. If you are currently active you will notice that the closer to your ideal weight you get, the better and stronger you will feel. Any exercise is better than none. Twenty minutes a day is not too much to allow yourself to add ten or more good years to your life.

Keep in mind that excessive weight can be a hindrance to any exercise that you choose. If you want to run, walk or hike and you find that your knees, hips, ankles or feet are hurting, it is probably because you are asking them to carry too much weight. Find something that you like, do it at a level that is reasonable and stick with it, or experiment. If you try enough things you can go on for quite a long time before you run out of options. Then, go back and review what you've tried. Maybe you can modify or combine techniques to suit your own unique character.

Start the Journey, Gently

Reward is a great motivator. So I say, let's reward ourselves. Treat yourself to a massage, a manicure or a pedicure. It doesn't have to be expensive. Sometimes if you shop around you can find very reasonable massage rates or just 1/2 an hour massages. Relax and be pampered.

I love the smell of scented candles and soft music to relax me, change my mood. You could even tie the massage into a reward for good behavior. You don't have to make it a strict connection. In other words, don't say, "I only get a massage IF I lose ten pounds." Say, "If I change my attitude or lose any weight at all, I will enjoy this great reward!"

On nice days, get out and walk! Walk around your neighborhood, meeting your neighbors. Find a nice trail in the hills, or along the beach. Take someone with you. Walking and talking does make the exercise time seem to fly. By the time you are done talking you would be surprised how far you have walked.

The Tea Ceremony

As for relaxing, I've always had a special love of sharing a cup of tea with a friend. Many cultures have elevated this simple act to a level of supreme importance. The English have a daily teatime. Some Japanese have made the tea ceremony a religious expression.

When I enjoy a cup of tea, I also enjoy a small cookie or two. Try it and let the tea metabolize the cookie for you!

Besides your nutritional needs, a relaxed moment with a friend can do wonders for your state of mind. As I previously wrote in the story, *The Mended Cup*, this is the way that women have been avoiding the need for psychiatrists and therapists for many decades.

Barbara is a published author and journalist. Her short story, "The Mended Cup" *appears in the collection,* A Cup of Comfort for Women, *published by Adams Media Corporation. She is co-writer of the blog:* Bifocal Reviews *(a link to these appear on the Vision-Revision wiki WebBook) and will be releasing her first novel, based-upon a true story entitled,* Through the Window *in 2012.*

Water for Meditation/It's Elemental

by Gordon Richiusa

(From a booklet and an insert in the original, Go Tao Chi)

What can I say about the importance of water, the ocean and the phenomenon of Wave Riding that has not already been said? Years ago, I wrote a book that was filled with photos of waves and excerpts from interviews that were conducted while surfing. I always took my journalistic curiosity with me wherever I went. I would paddle out on my own board and ask the nearest stranger questions about surfing that pertained to the five principles. Today, we hear the term "soul surfing" as it relates to seeing surfing as a spiritual endeavor.

The point I was trying to make by my interviews (which, admittedly I probably had not succeeded in accomplishing) was that riding and, indeed appreciating the waves on the shore of any ocean can help one to get in touch with the Flow of Life. Besides the fact that water is essential for the existence of life (after air, it is the most important ingredient for human survival), there have been a number of studies conducted and proofs offered that being in and around water is beneficial on a number of levels.

There was recently even a photographer (Masaru Emoto in his The Messages of Water) who showed with microphotography, that the way human beings "felt" or the thoughts they were expressing—even the words they chose to speak aloud—actually affected the molecular structure of the water molecule. As you know, water is one element that can be experienced in three forms, solid, liquid and gas.

There are a group of people who believe humans are closely related to dolphins and whales because of what is known as the "diving reflex." All a human being has to do is have his face touch water and their heart rate slows, making them require less oxygen. Another group is a proponent of "water birthing" whereby women give birth in water because it is a more tranquil environment than a hospital room. In addition, a baby (like a dolphin or whale) will not try to breathe until their nose hits the open air.

In any event, water has been an important part of my life since a very young age and I've continued to practice Go-Tao-Chi on the shore as a personal favorite for enhancing my spiritual awareness. To illustrate our Five Principles points more clearly let's look at how humans interact with water as a way to see how we relate to the world around us.

Swimming, for instance is NOT a natural activity. Human beings (and our close relatives of monkeys, or apes who walk primarily on two legs) cannot swim without instruction. They must "learn the ways of swimming." The reason for this is simple physics. Every animal reaches "neutral buoyancy," at some point when immersed in water. That means that everything floats. The problem is that most four legged animals reach neutral buoyancy at a depth where they can still keep their heads above water in a position that is natural for them. Humans, unfortunately reach neutral buoyancy, with only the tops of their heads (if they are lucky) at the surface, and with their mouth underwater. This is due to the fact that their natural position is upright, on two legs. This is why it is easier to teach a baby to swim than an adult, and why four-legged animals will follow their mother directly into the water and swim easily. Four-legged animals, when them swim, are generally not doing anything differently than they would do on land. The Greek philosopher and mathematician, Archimedes realized that: "Any object, wholly or partially immersed in a fluid, is buoyed up by a force equal to the weight of the fluid displaced by the object." It is why a huge boat, made of concrete or steel can float. It must reach its neutral buoyancy point with its deck above the surface.

James E. "Doc" Counsilman, in his book *The Science of Swimming* demonstrated how important an understanding of the laws Newtonian Physics are in improving your swimming strokes. Everything from how friction and propulsion affect the stroke to "A body in motion tends to stay in motion," to the concept that some people are naturally going to be faster in the water, based entirely upon the fat content just below the skin. Nonetheless, it would not be an exaggeration to say that Doc Counsilman lived and died in the study to improve swimming.

I still swim several times a week and body-board or just sit by or run on or near water whenever I cannot get into it. Whenever I do get into water, whether I am swimming a particular stroke or just floating, I think about the "way of swimming and water" that I learned from reading Doc Counsilman's books. I also like to practice tai chi or yoga-like movements, just floating with my face just beneath the surface, so that my body calms, my heart rate slows and I am forced to control my breathing to a greater extent than I might with my body on dry land. There is a "right" way to interact with water that varies with the individual, the form of the water, and the ultimate purpose that one is trying to derive from the interaction. If you are trying to swim fast, then certain laws of physics are relevant and important. If you are diving or floating, then Archimedes' buoyancy principle is at work, whether you know it or not. If you simply are watching water spill over an embankment or lap against a shore or fall frozen in snowflake form, your awareness is always enhanced by a combination of concepts and experience.

Finally, when I think back on my most memorable moments in my lifetime, being inside a "tube" of a wave, with the accompanying sound, sights and physical stimulation is something that is etched into the core of my being as being transcendental. The brief moment of unique sights, sounds, feelings that are a direct reward for the conscious choices, and motivations that led me to that spot in the wave are a gift of life that even the most stubborn, hard-headed human can appreciate.

Note from author/editor: The following is an excerpt from Jhoon Rhee's Trutopia. *For you academics, note the similarities between Jhoon Rhee's philosophy and those attributed to other great philosophers such as Aristotle and Socrates. Also, whenever you like, try to replace the words "martial arts" or "Tae Kwon Do" with "success" or others familiar to you in your own disciplines. We cannot begin to express our gratitude to Mr. Rhee for allowing us to include these pages in our text.*

My Vision for the Third Millennium

By Grandmaster Jhoon Rhee

We, the Martial Artists, citizens of the world, hereby declare the "Lead by Example Action Philosophy" to the world. We all know that a picture is worth a 1000 words, but we also must know that an action is worth a 1000 pictures. The "Lead by Example Action Philosophy" is designed to inspire all people to be more enlightened; to ensure effective children's education for family unity; and to promote cultural diversity for universal harmony. The "Lead by Example Action Philosophy" can be achieved through "Joy of Discipline"—a mental and physical exercise program that can lead us to achieve "100 Years of Wisdom in a Body of 21 Years Young," the foundation for a happy global society.

The "Lead by Example Action Philosophy" is a new social awakening campaign for a perfect global society in the Third Millennium. It is not a religion, but recognizes a Supreme Intelligence as the origin of life and happiness. People constantly move to avoid pain or to seek joy and comfort.

Therefore, the universal purpose of life, unquestionably, is happiness. The ultimate value for happiness is Love; only Beauty triggers the love emotion; and only Truth beautifies the human heart. Therefore, when I am truthful, my heart is beautiful; when my heart is beautiful, people love me; when people love me, I am happy.

Conversely, when I deceive, my heart is ugly; when my heart is ugly, people hate me; when people hate me, I am unhappy. Therefore, a truthful way of life is not only good, but also wise; deceiving is not only wrong, but also foolish. Truth, Beauty, and Love are the three basic elements of Good that we must live by daily. Deceit, ugliness, and hatred are three basic elements of evil that we must recognize but never practice. All thoughts of Truth, Beauty, and Love secrete a positive brain substance, Beta Endorphin, for better health and happiness, but thoughts of deceit, ugliness, and hatred secrete adrenaline, which leads to stress that can cause fatal diseases.

Everyone is born to be happy with each breath of life. We all deserve the most joyful social environment for absolute global happiness. The foundation for a happy society is perfect human character, exercising true freedom approved by one's conscience, and never practicing false freedom licensed by selfish animal instinct. People of the Third Millennium must be perfect human beings, defined by never making mistakes knowingly, harmful to none, and beneficial to all. Therefore, as a martial artist, I must first develop a perfect body as the temple for a perfect mind.

An ideal human being is one who has achieved an education consisting of three basic human qualities—Strength, Honesty, and Knowledge. The purpose of knowledge is to take action, for knowing does not make things happen, but actions always do. All parents of the

Third Millennium must become teachers for their children, not by words alone but also by their actions, for children are born to learn not only by listening but more by watching deeds of adults. Consistent good behavior and spontaneous action come only by skills and good habits.

Three Golden Rules for parents and teachers to help children develop many good skills and habits are: (1) Lead by Example. (2) Never fail to correct their mistakes with a smile until good habits are formed. (3) Lead by Example continually.

Therefore, I recite My Four Daily Affirmations to reaffirm my daily commitment to achieve 100 years of wisdom in a body 21 years young, as follows:

1. I like myself because I always take action to make good things happen.

2. I am humanly perfect because I never make a mistake knowingly.

3. I am wise because I always learn something good everyday.

4. I am happy that I am me because I always choose to be happy.

"Therefore, I am one of the wise, humanly perfect, active, and happy centers of the universe." Jhoon Rhee

Seven Qualities of a Champion

A. Martial Arts as Action Philosophy

When I first became a Taekwondo instructor, I claimed that my martial art is a philosophy, which can be very instrumental in developing our youth through mental discipline and physical conditioning. However, I had a difficult time justifying to myself how punching and kicking could be a philosophy. In the early 1970s, I was writing a column for Blackbelt magazine. The editor called on me to write an article to justify Taekwondo as a philosophy. I felt I was in trouble because I did not know what to say. During three months of research, I was able to develop my article, "Seven Qualities of a Champion," which has gone on to become quite popular among martial artists of various other styles.

Psychologists say that logic may not always activate an emotion, but actions always do. The most effective way to create a desired mental state is by a physiological activity which parallels this desired state. In other words, our state of mind is caused, not only by thoughts, but also through physiologies such as spoken words, actions, and chosen body postures. When I ask my audience: "Please try to be sad," almost everyone lowers their heads and shoulders. If I ask: "Try to be excited," then, nearly everyone raises their heads and straightens their body postures.

Dr. Bernie Siegel is the author of a book called Love, Medicine and Miracles. He is a surgeon who has worked with cancer patients using psychological imaging. What is fascinating is how closely the mind and body are related. For instance, he tells how twelve cancer patients were all given a pill and told it was a chemotherapy pill. However, six of the patients were given only a placebo. Guess what happened? All twelve patients, including those only given placebos, had their hair fall out. In other words, because these people believed the pill would cause their hair to fall out, this was the message their minds gave to their bodies, and their bodies reacted to it. Isn't that amazing?

From these observations, I was reassured that martial arts can be "action philosophies" which can help change our children's behavior. The teaching essence of martial arts must be philosophy, for martial arts without philosophy is merely street fighting.

Now let us examine how physical qualities can enhance human qualities, which can be applied to our daily living. In a champion of martial arts and of life, we find corresponding parallel qualities.

There are seven basic physical qualities that are developed through martial arts training. These physical qualities can be transformed into human qualities because the body and mind are as inseparable as heat and light in a flame. It is an important psychological discovery that a motion triggers an emotion as much as an emotion triggers a motion. In other words, we are happy when we sing; also we sing when we are happy. In order to become a true champion of life, and in the martial arts, we must develop the following human qualities by making a habit of positive actions.

B. Seven Qualities Of a Champion

1. Power/Knowledge/Capital Power

One will never become a champion in martial arts without developing power—developing mental and physical strength. We all have the potential for genius, and everyone can become an expert in at least one field, through which we can serve others for mutual happiness. There are two kinds of knowledge: that of worldly matters and of mental matters. Knowledge of worldly matters enables us to do something for ourselves, first, and then we can share it with others. Knowledge of mental matters enables us to develop a good character for better human relationship with others.

Complementing knowledge of the mind is knowledge of worldly matters, which show us the way to intellectual strength. As we generate our physical strength through development of our muscles by daily exercise, we must also develop mental strength through development of our mental muscles in daily mental exercise—positive thinking, memorization, analysis, creativity, and problem solving.

A healthy body provides only for physical comfort but not for peace of mind or happiness.

Honesty may bring peace of mind but not necessarily happiness, the ultimate purpose of life. An honest person may not harm anyone but without knowledge or skill, he or she cannot contribute to society.

True happiness comes from being physically free to do the things the mind desires. Mental and physical strengths together can provide us with the means to actualize our desires. A person is a product of their upbringing and education, with a seemingly limitless inborn capacity to learn if only one understands how to unlock his or her full potential.

As our bodies grow, so do our minds. One of the main causes of unhappiness is the daily mistakes we make either knowingly (crimes) or unknowingly (accidents); either way, they do hurt us. Through education, the human race has done much to improve its economic standards. I believe that everyone is born a genius and has the potential to achieve success if one has the right attitude and the desire to succeed.

"A genius is made by one percent inspiration and 99 percent perspiration." —Thomas Edison

I am very happy that our profession, teaching the martial arts, is recognized as one of the most beautiful arts by the general public, especially when its movements are synchronized with music. John Adams, early in his professional life, implied that the purpose of studying is to enhance arts for the ultimate fulfillment of human happiness. We, as martial arts champions, must develop our powers by strengthening the body, heart, and mind, in order to effectively and efficiently learn how to continually apply our craft. The late legendary UCLA basketball Coach John Wooden, age 98, said: "When I am through learning, then I am through."

As long as we live, we should never stop learning. So, let us cultivate power by developing strength in the body, honesty in the heart, and knowledge in the mind. We can increase our knowledge in the mind through constant learning, by listening to our conscience and reason, and from accumulating our knowledge of worldly matters by paying close attention to our teachers and the world around us. With both inner and outer forms of knowledge, we will develop strength within ourselves and be able to positively influence those around us.

As we martial artists develop a daily habit of exercising our muscles, to become champions, we also must develop a daily learning habit in order to become human champions. Those who develop daily habits of exercising and of learning surely will realize financial success as well as the true confidence and pride necessary for a happy life.

2. Quickness/Alertness/Awareness

The word "Accu-punch" was coined while I trained Muhammad Ali for his title-defending match against British champion Richard Dunn in Munich, Germany in 1976. I defined "Accu-punch" as a punch executed at the moment I decided to punch—a punch of the body and mind in synchronization. There should be no time gap between the decision and execution of a punch. This will not only eliminate telegraphed motion, but also increase acceleration and enormously increase power. I have been applying this principle in my daily life—"Never procrastinate."

When I conduct my martial arts seminars, I enjoy doing a punching demonstration with the help of two or three volunteers from the audience. I ask them to block a punch aimed at their faces. No one has ever been able to block this punch; although once by luck a gentleman did it in Hawaii. The truth is it is almost impossible to block, not only because my punch is fast, but also because I understand the psychological principle of "Accu- punch." This principle is to strike at the same instant the decision to punch is made.

When you see a red light while driving, you cannot step on the brake pedal at the same moment the light changes. It takes time to communicate—your eyes tell the brain, and your brain tells your foot to step on the brake. The length of time required to react is called "human reaction time." This lag is the reason why, when designing traffic lights, how long the yellow light lasts is determined by the speed limit and the width of each intersection. To be a champion in life, we must not only be able to physically react quickly, we must also develop the ability to think quickly when meeting challenges and solving problems in daily life.

Obviously, it is a very important principle for all fighters to punch without being blocked.

The name of the game in a fight is to hit the enemy before he can hit you. Staying one step ahead of your opponent is the key to success. We may have no control over the techniques our opponents throw at us, but what is within our control is how we counterattack or initiate an offensive tactic.

By the same token, we have no control over our daily

challenges; however, we do control how we prepare in advance and react to each incident. It is our attitude that determines the outcome of everything in our daily lives. Just as you will miss most targets without a habit of responding quickly, those who make a habit of procrastinating will not succeed in life because they are thieves of their own time.

So, let us develop a habit of thinking fast and staying one step ahead of the competition by always being prepared in daily life, just as we develop speed to stay ahead of an opponent in order to become a champion in martial arts. Remember, we should never procrastinate, for procrastinators are thieves of their own time.

3. Timing/ Punctuality/ On Time Delivery

In order to become a martial arts champion, one must develop near-perfect timing. Developing speed and power is not enough to become a champion. Being the quickest and strongest does not necessarily equate with success, unless that individual learns to act at the appropriate moments. During sparring, there is no time to think. Every move has to be made at the right moment in order for it to connect with the opponent. Through constant practice, we will be able to throw kicks and punches at the correct targets at the right moment.

By the same token, in order to become a champion in

life, we must develop a habit of choosing the right moment and acting appropriately for success. This includes developing the daily habit of punctuality by honoring appointments made with our family, friends, peers, and other associates. As George Washington said, "Discipline is the soul of an army."

The discipline to respect time is one way to develop self-respect, the first step toward respect for parents, teachers, and peers. There are many who are capable, yet fail in life due to the lack of discipline in their proper use of time. We are limited by time and space and must respect both of these by being punctual. With the habit of being punctual, we develop a good reputation and create credibility—qualities which are the basis for success in life. The expression, "To succeed, one must be at the right place at the right time," sums up the importance of timing in becoming a champion in life.

In my senior year at the University of Texas, one of my teachers said, "When you get your job, develop a habit of being at your office five minutes before work starts in the morning, and leaving your office five minutes after closing time; your boss sure will love you for that, and you will be the one to be promoted when the next vacant position is open."

So, let us develop punctuality in daily life, just as we develop a sense of good timing to become a champion in martial arts.

4. Endurance/ Perseverance/ Persistence

In the martial arts, a champion must train to develop stamina—a form of cardiovascular and muscular endurance. The Jhoon Rhee Institute created the "double-counter," a beginner's sparring training program, which is a method to develop a student's determination to win.

This program creates the habit of delivering a second or third counter when our attacks are blocked and counterattacked. Frequently, we do not succeed on the first attempt to counter our opponent's attack, but we usually do on the second or third try.

Thomas Edison, the greatest inventor in modern history, spoke words of wisdom after failing so many times in his experiments to develop the carbon-impregnated filament used in the first incandescent light-bulb. After 5,000 experiments, a young journalist asked why he persisted in his experiments after all these failures. Edison replied: "Young man, you don't understand how the world works. I have not failed at all. I have successfully identified 5,000 ways that do not work. This just puts me 5,000 ways closer to the way it will work."

Depending on the individual, a sense of persistence can change not only the destiny of one person but all of human history. Marvin White, one of my brown belt students, was born with fetal thalidomide syndrome—having only one leg, two elbows and only one thumb on the left elbow. He used to come to watch classes at one of our Taekwondo studios in Stafford, Virginia, where his younger brother had become a student. One day Master Ken Carlson, the head instructor, told Marvin that if he wanted to, he too could learn martial arts. He did not believe Master Carlson at first, but Master Carlson's persistent attempts finally persuaded Marvin to give it a try. A year later, Marvin could break two boards with his spinning 360 degree wheel kick, two boards and one cinder block with his elbow, and one board held up head-high using a jump front kick. After his demonstrations, he touched many hearts, including mine, by saying to his audience: "I am not 'Marvelous Marvin,' but I am Happy Marvin. If I can be happy, there is no reason why anyone cannot be happy."

Persistence is meeting challenges, but it also includes the ability to develop and maintain a consistent level of success. Establishing consistency can be manifested through the universal practice of maintaining perfect attendance—arriving on-time to work or school each and every day.

Perfect attendance is emblematic of this principle because it shows the ability of the individual to give priority to what is important—their job or school. In order to establish perfect attendance, these individuals must not get distracted by lesser priorities or put themselves at risk of getting sick. While momentary successes may be difficult to achieve, long-term goals such as perfect attendance can be done but require persistent effort. For instance, Hall of Fame baseball player Cal Ripken, Jr. was an outstanding shortstop and third baseman. However, he is known as "Iron Man" because he consistently maintained a high level of performance and kept himself healthy for 2,632 consecutive games—a span of over 16 years!

So, let us develop a sense of persistence in daily life just as we develop a sense of endurance to become a champion in the martial arts.

5. Balance/ Rationality/ Stability

In order to become a martial arts champion, we must have a good sense of physical balance; when you lose your balance in a fight, you may lose the fight. When you are kicking with one leg, you have only one leg to balance your body. Through disciplined training one must develop this sense of balance to become a martial arts champion.

I have repeated the motto of "strength in the body,

honesty in the heart, and knowledge in the mind" many times in my writings, because our goal is to make all children of the next generation able to meet the qualifications for true humanhood: strength, honesty, and knowledge—a humanly perfect character.

A person of wisdom and character who is without strength will not be able to function physically; a person of wisdom and strength without character will be dangerous; and a person of character and strength but without knowledge will not be in high demand by any society. Therefore, it is our duty to build balanced qualities of health, character, and wisdom starting from the earliest age possible, before children become contaminated by negative social environments.

To be a champion in the martial arts, one must develop proficiency in the ability to use both hands and both feet. It is not sufficient to develop a dominant or strong side for punching or kicking. This will not only limit the possibilities of the individual, it will also create a dependency, which can be exploited if the dominant side becomes injured.

Furthermore, a martial arts champion must be expert in using both feet and hands—four weapons are certainly greater than only one or two! By this same token, a champion in life needs to successfully balance good health due to proper diet (eating moderate quantities of good-quality food), exercise and rest, and by enjoying hobbies, as well as enjoying successes in interpersonal relations and at work or school.

We all have to balance our checkbooks. In the business world, our financial statements must be balanced. Families work on balancing their budgets. Our government is run on a basis of checks and balances and must continuously strive to balance the national budget. Politicians of any nation must balance their power by balancing executive, legislative, and judiciary branches of government.

Let us develop a sense of balance by cultivating strength in the body, honesty in the heart, and knowledge in the mind, just as a martial artist must also develop a sense of physical balance by training both sides of the body and by standing on one leg at a time.

6. Flexibility/ Gentleness/ Adaptability

Flexibility is one of the most important physical qualities for martial artists, especially when attempting to execute high kicks. More importantly, good flexibility helps prevent muscle and ligament injuries and helps us maintain our physical youth. By the same token, an open mind is at the core of becoming a champion in life.

The nature of water is the best example of the kind of

flexible character, which all people should learn. (Isn't it interesting that our bodies happen to be mostly composed of water?) Water is shapeless, colorless, odorless, and tasteless. When it is poured in a round container, its shape becomes round; square in a square container. When you add red dye, it becomes red water; blue water with blue dye and yellow, black, and so on.

When we drink water, it becomes our blood, hormones, tears, and many other forms of liquid, which the human body needs. Water becomes wine with grapes or some other fruits; when it is mixed with soap, it becomes soapy water that can clean up dirt. When water is mixed with sand and cement, it becomes buildings.

Rain water comes from high heaven yet always seeks the lowest places on earth, to wet all the dry land, to give life to the plant kingdom which in turn gives life to the animal kingdom, including all of humankind. Then, the water as vapor quietly disappears into heaven again without claiming any credit.

Most dogmatic religions have their own fixed shapes like hard and cold ice. They claim to be the only truth by denying the beliefs of other religions. Rigidly conforming our beliefs to any religion's dogma freezes our potential and confines it into that religion's prescribed block of ice.

Instead, let us all strive to become like water – limitless in our potential.

Today, too many conflicts are caused by rigid, close-minded people who lack any understanding of others. We should always be open-minded and respect others. One of the major social problems is the differences in the beliefs among people who follow dogmatic religions. Many people are taught, "Unless you believe in my God, you will go to Hell." This is really a narrow-minded view and very offensive to other people. I know people believe in the freedom of religion, yet some still believe that those who do not believe their religion will be damned for eternity.

I tried to find out the reason why some religions glorify suicide to please God; I discovered the reason. Some religions have taught people to live and die to honor God ever since human history began. I am not sure this teaching is the will of God. If God's love is unconditional, the teaching has to be changed. I am sure that most parents with these religious beliefs must be living with constant worry that their children may commit suicide.

I envisioned that God is very sad when people kill themselves for God, just as we the physical parents will be heartbroken if our children kill themselves to please their parents—us. We must understand God is not selfish as we are. Although people are selfish, no parents demand their children to live and die for them. If God's love is unconditional, I believe God must be telling us: "Children, I did not create you for My own glory at all; I created you for your own happy living. Don't worry about Me at all; just enjoy your life by loving one another. Besides, there is nothing you can do for Me anyway. Loving your brothers and sisters, my beloved children, is the only way you can honor Me. As Benjamin Franklin said: The most acceptable service we render to Him is in doing good to His other children."

> *A man is born gentle and weak.*
> *At death, he is hard and stiff.*
> *Green plants are tender and filled with sap.*
> *At death, they are withered and dry.*
> *Therefore, the stiff and unbending is the disciple of death,*
> *And the gentle and yielding is the disciple of life."*
> — Lao Tzu

Maintaining mental flexibility also broadens our ability to find unexpected moments of learning and success and, coupled with our timing, can enable us to benefit even from the most unlikely of occasions or unexpected sources of inspiration. For instance, open- minded teachers are able to improve their abilities to teach by learning from students who may pose a strange question or cause the teacher to rethink an approach to solving a problem. We call these instances "teachable moments."

A champion in the martial arts, too, must keep an open mind in order to continue to grow and progress, especially after becoming a Black Belt, because having finally achieved this rank may become an excuse for complacency. Becoming a Black Belt in a particular style of the martial arts is merely the beginning of a continuing, life-long journey of learning.

Earning a Black Belt means the individual has demonstrated proficiency in the development of basics and in numerous extensions of those basics. As with students of any other rank, Black Belts must be receptive to the lessons that their senior Black Belts may provide as well as stay sensitive to "teachable moments" that might occur when interacting with peers or more junior students.

Let us tap into our limitless potential by actualizing the principle of water and by maintaining or cultivating that open-mindedness which expands our horizons. As Lao Tzu expounded, the closed-mind is the principle of stagnation and death. To be champions in life and the martial arts, we must maintain mental and physical flexibility in order to keep our minds and bodies young and vibrant.

7. Posture/ Honesty/ Business Integrity

In martial arts, upright posture lends a balanced beauty to the art. This beauty is appreciated not only by the martial artists but also by the general public. As the standard of physical beauty—symmetry and relative proportions—is generally universal, the inner beauty of a person with good posture—correct alignment—also is universal.

The martial arts champion must develop good posture, which requires good flexibility and persistence in order to correctly align the body. Developing good posture in the martial arts has aesthetic appeal, but more importantly, it is essential for efficient and effective application of techniques—whether it is for combat (sparring or self-defense) or for performing public demonstrations. Having bad posture will hinder and weaken the power and speed of a movement, minimizing its impact.

As it is vital for martial artists, good posture is also key to becoming a champion in life. Posture is the outward manifestation of a person's character. Aligned posture represents a person's character being correct and upright through honesty, while crooked posture represents flawed character. There is a reason for the phrase "upstanding citizen" being associated with being of good character. From a physical standpoint, developing good posture is critical for maintaining our physical youth. Posture—whether aligned or slouched—directly affects the health of our spine, which could mean the difference between aging quickly or aging gracefully. If we develop a habit of standing, sitting, and lying down in alignment with our natural spinal curvature, our spines will stay healthier and keep our bodies upright for years to come.

As aforementioned, the position of our bodies impacts our mood: when I ask my audience to physically demonstrate sadness, their bodies slouch, and when I ask them to demonstrate happiness, they become upright. In addition to improving mood, good posture improves our social status and image.

I have spent ten years researching how to invent spine-correcting shoulder straps.

Children's postures are more crooked than ever due to how they sit at their computers.

Some children are glued to their computers for fun and games. Some are there for studies. I hope someday all governments will make an invention like the shoulder straps available for children, on whose shoulders the future of their countries must be carried.

Let us re-discover and maintain good posture, not only

for our health, social standing and good looks, but also as a manifestation of our mental discipline while we develop good character through truthfulness.

An Explanation of the Five Principles of FASST/Dux Ryu

By Frank Dux

My words are often twisted. I am grateful for this opportunity to explain how my FASST program is consistent with the Five Principles of Everything.

What does FASST stand for?

Focus—The Mindset; concentrated effort; decisions made in advance; the ability to utilize fear and decide without distraction or hesitation on a course of action: (i.e. centered to the point of being unwavering in the face of overwhelming odds, death, etc.).

Action—Voluntary or intended behavior as opposed to forced behavior/being Proactive vs. Reactive. Those definable observable acts that demonstrate ones commitment: (i.e. physically engaging in conflict not out of panic but wisdom).

Skill—Individual characteristics gained through experience and training. The physical capabilities one possess: e.g. explosive speed, endurance, trauma conditioning, timing, range, reflexive and instinctive reaction as well as proactive/offensive limitations, etc.

Strategy—Long term aims: the ability to develop, create, adapt, perceive; to devise a plan of action to achieve a goal/result,

Tactics—"The toolbox" is the methodology of finding and implementing the means to achieve particular immediate short-term aims. (The science of organizing and maneuvering in battle, to achieve a limited and immediate aim i.e. using the set maneuvers for defending oneself from a slashing knife or a front thrust kick).

A Science for the Individual/A Personalized Approach

Using FASST/Dux Ryu when fighting, one can adapt and combine individually learned techniques—those, which best serve one's individual strengths and weaknesses. In place of reacting, one is acting by controlling the rhythm and pace of every fighting action in one's favor, which can be achieved by one's mastery over the angles of evasion and attack—the laws governing footwork and strikes.

Thusly, one is avoiding the pitfalls like that of the five foot tall, three hundred pound, obese man or woman who has enrolled in a rigid traditional martial arts class for self-defense where it is expected that one must conform, arguably to keep the style pure. This requirement ignores the apparent fact that one is physically incapable of utilizing the style to its fullest potential. For instance: being taught no alternative but to attempt to kick above the waist by which to defend oneself from an attacker, because the mastery of kicking is the central focus of the self-defense system, does not suit all practitioners. Unable to optimize one's full abilities, logic dictates that these practitioners are always going to be left more vulnerable and limited than is necessary.

In the case of FASST/Dux Ryu—while kicking is taught—the vast arsenal of techniques, topic range, and the flexibility of the system will enable the same obese man or woman to discover and optimize his or her weight and size in a manner by which to be exploited. For example, the obese weight becomes a tactical advantage when this practitioner is now concentrating on power punching, grappling and choke-out techniques where his size provides him an advantage over a less formidable or sizable aggressor.

As well, the opposite holds true as a smaller, frailer person would have little or a poor chance of trying to strong-arm and wrestle someone to the ground who is twice his size. However, the smaller size and wiry stature makes him exceptionally deadly in a lethal situation where he could attack the lower extremities, puncturing the femoral artery with ease, producing death in even a giant of a man within seconds.

The FASST/Dux Ryu trainee does not conform to the system nor must he abandon what he knows or the system of martial arts or defensive tactics system he follows. The FASST/Dux Ryu system is specifically designed to meet the trainee's individual needs and abilities as well as make him keenly aware of not only the inherent vulnerabilities he possesses but how to determine, in a split second, the strengths of his aggressors—which are to be avoided to prevail.

In short, FASST/Dux Ryu is a compilation of the Secrets of Warriorship. It is the amplifier, the natural steroid, the edge, the catalyst to ignite and fire up the spirit to compliment and accentuate and expand one's spirituality, physicality, and mental capabilities and skills. Thusly, it produces measurable results far exceeding personal expectations in the shortest time possible.

A Science for Everyone—A New Methodology

That FASST/Dux Ryu is the compilation of the Secrets of Warriorship makes it particularly well suited to assisting the already trained martial artist or defensive tactics practitioner who is experiencing a lull or plateau in their performance and growth. With FASST/Dux Ryu's breakthrough technology, insights, and secrets, one does not have to throw away or abandon one's style or prior knowledge. Just the opposite holds true as all styles are connected by virtue of human biomechanics. The whole premise of FASST/Dux Ryu is based upon the integration and application of technology and education of laws and principles that better enable, fortify, and teach one to apply and integrate his prior experience and training in a superior manner that best compliments the practitioner's style.

FASST is the product of a lifetime of study and a unique insightful experience. Success or failure is solely based upon one's new ability to fully comprehend and utilize the Secrets of Warriorship as identified and codified by martial arts legend, Hanshi Dux.

While tactics and abilities will vary from individual to individual based on the above facts, it is because of the methodology, education materials, and technology being employed by FASST/Dux Ryu that the same empirical rules and principles apply, linking all trainees similarly. However, FAAST/Dux Ryu is not solely confined in its training methodology to only incorporate or primarily rely upon a set of theoretical or empirically defined movements in and of themselves as in alternative martial arts styles and defensive tactics programs.

As stated before, FAAST/Dux Ryu is not absent in addressing the mindset and/or academics involved, especially regarding threat level 4—lethal confrontations. Typically, the two subjects of a prepared spirit and academics are abandoned or are unincorporated by alternative training/defensive tactics systems, abandoning their students to their own devices.

A Focus on Efficiency—Explosive Speed and Power

Another differentiating factor that separates it from traditional training courses is that the FASST/Dux Ryu system is of the belief that, while a predetermined combination of reflexive movements increases instinct and response time, it also sets limits on flexibility and adaptability and makes one predictable in real combat—vulnerable to attack in light of the fact that combat is always changing and will take on a life of its own due to environmental constrictions and a host of other variables. These variables cannot be anticipated in advance by those practiced responses/techniques that one is expected to utilize when threatened.

One of the first Secrets of Warriorship is as follows: "The effectiveness of an aggressor is chiefly determined by the aggressor's capability to predict one's responses and counter/engage those responses with devastating results." Hence, explosive speed and power take precedence over flowery fluidity or predictable, stylized form. Efficiency and ferocity—explosive speed and power—are the main components that dictate what is and is not useful by FASST/Dux Ryu standards and are the long established evidence proving that the Secrets of Warriorship are hard at work.

For example, where others who are prancing around wielding a blade will tend to slash, utilizing FAAST/Dux Ryu technology of the angles of evasion in relation to the angles of attack, one is enabled to thrust by vectoring in footwork to create the shortest distance and time to negate any attack as fast as possible by being the one delivering the first decisive fatal blow. Increasing endurance by expending less energy—explosive speed and efficiency of motion makes it viable for a FASST/Dux Ryu trainee to combat multiple attackers. The ability to respond and dispatch a lethal threat quickly enables the trainee to come to the aid of teammates or others in danger of being overpowered, injured, or killed.

Spirit, Mind, and Body—Key Aspects of a Person

Another aspect that differentiates FASST/Dux Ryu from alternative martial arts and defensive tactics courses in the ways they are and have been taught is that the FASST/Dux Ryu training philosophy is truly grounded in the Secrets of Warriorship. It begins by identifying and then developing in synchronicity a training program that addresses the three critical characteristic attributes of a warrior: spirit, mind, and body. These three characteristics must be superior to those possessed by any aggressor, principally if one is to be truly centered to neutralize a lethal threat.

The characteristics of spirit, mind, and body are the grave variables that, if impacted, will determine all outcomes in any form of conflict. It is the means by which to be grounded in handling everyday life adversity. However, one's examination of spirit, mind, and body is best known as being employed to dissect an aggressor and to discover their vulnerabilities in relation to one's own. Thereby, one formulates a proper strategy and employs the appropriate techniques to control the situation and resolve conflict in one's favor. This is the way of the FASST/Dux Ryu trainee and the peaceful warrior that the great Chinese strategist Sun Tzu describes as "the ultimate form of warriorship."

Most martial arts and defensive tactics systems, when they do address these three attributes, profess the concept of harmonizing as always in the order of mind, body, and spirit, which is left generally open to interpretation if queried. Whereas, by FASST/Dux Ryu philosophy, these individuals have the very order mixed up as it is always about having the proper spirit or mindset first. The mind, which is most often confused by the ill trained to mean the mindset, but which actually represents the academics of combat and body, is also misinterpreted by the majority of today's martial arts practitioners to be only a reference to one's physicality, neglecting to include potential as in the body of their work of past and future, or as in how their character is perceived by others and themselves.

The actual techniques for harmonizing spirit, mind, and body posses proven results, but unfortunately are not being taught in the dojos and are now seemingly lost due to circumstances beyond the average martial arts instructor's control or understanding. However, FASST/Dux Ryu incorporates the old lost ways with the new. Unlike other systems that have become watered down to meet modern day commercial needs and consumer demands of instant gratification, or just as a matter of the passing of time and knowledge lost from one generation to the next, everything in FASST/Dux Ryu in its conveyance of the Secrets of Warriorship leaves no concept or principle left open to interpretation, assumption, or change, as exemplified by the way these warrior characteristics of spirit, mind, and body are defined by FASST/Dux Ryu:

Spirit—The spirit is one's mindset—one's focus—which is the proactive versus reactive ability to utilize fear and be committed to engage in conflict to the point of being unwavering in the face of overwhelming odds.

Mind—The mind is the academics—knowledge of strategy and tactics—and the ability to create, adapt, perceive, and alter a course of action to produce a desired result.

Body—The body is one's explosive speed and the physical capabilities one possesses: endurance, trauma conditioning, timing, range, reflexive and instinctive reaction, as well as proactive/offensive limitations. The body is the essence of a person and what he projects as a member of society, as in one's body of accomplishments and work (merchant, artisan, doctor). It is also how one is to be perceived by others—that which the Japanese samurai calls "face."

One can be the fastest, strongest, and most skilled opponent (body) but, without the skill to develop the proper will (spirit), or the ability to develop the academics to determine when and when not to strike (mind), all is vanity. Akin to this scenario is the scene in the motion picture Raider's of The Lost Ark where a sword wielding antagonist is so consumed by his own ego (poor spirit) in showing off his awesome abilities with two swords (body), that he loses sight of the advantage of the surprise attack (mind), only to end up nonchalantly and comically shot to death by the merely annoyed protagonist, Indiana Jones.

On its face, with little or no attention being given to the development and enhancement of the human spirit and/or the scientific academics—especially surrounding lethal combat—and by one only concentrating chiefly on physicality (i.e. how to grapple, kick, or punch), this all makes for a bitter game of chance. A vulnerable spirit and indecisive mind (no strategy) is prone to produce predictable responses and reactions instead of actions, which in lethal confrontations puts one at an extreme disadvantage, and which usually produces another predictable result: death.

"I've trained my whole life and thought I'd seen and practically done it all, from Judo/Jujitsu, Jeet Kun Do, Ninjutsu, Kung Fu, etc. The very first FASST/Dux Ryu seminar I took affected me and everyone I know who has ever attended—dramatically. As the Dux system is as he says, not theoretical but empirical, comprised of real combat tested and proven tactics with scientific reproducible results, that make up new principles and a new biomechanical technology, one that is not just another quick fix or empty promise adaptation of the run-of-the-mill classical martial arts or the so-called latest defensive tactics system or any combination therein. As a direct result, it increased my performance after I thought it couldn't get any better; so significantly, that now martial arts masters that are my senior, with twice the time in experience in the martial arts, are turning to me for training advice. In one case, one well-known master's students, seeing the overwhelming change I was able to instill in my students using FASST, are now demanding changes in their training from him! Frank Dux's FASST program is what a martial art is supposed to be." — Sensei Sky Benson

NOTE: Sky Benson is a long time student of Frank Dux, was instructed by Gordon Richiusa when Gordon worked for Hanshi Dux, and is the webmaster for the FASST website found at: www.fasstduxryu.com.

Health, Healing and Recovery

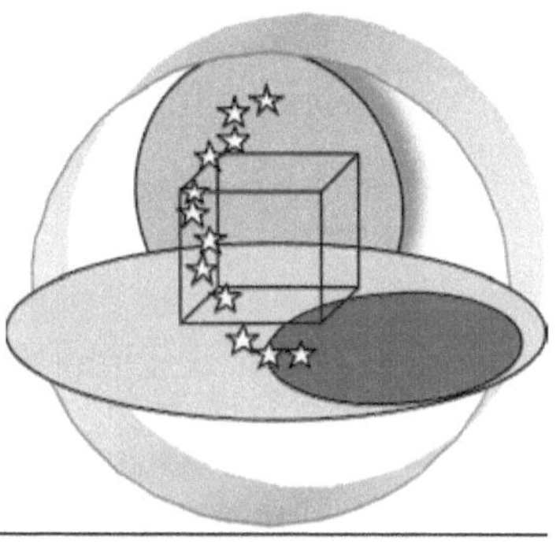

by Maria Arvelo

The year I turned 30 was a pivotal point in my life. I had completed 10 years of metaphysical study, successfully confronting barriers and obstacles that had hindered my ability to achieve a deeply desired "dream piece". In the light of my success with a deepened sense of appreciation for life, myself and for the accompanying joy, I was gifted with knowledge I previously could not know. This knowledge was a secret – a secret that I kept from myself for my entire life. I had been sexually abused. The fear, terror, and betrayal I could not know as a five year old, I could tolerate knowing as a thirty year old. Acquiring this knowledge, though knowable was still too intense — shattering my understanding of almost all I knew to be true. I was catapulted from basking in the light into darkness and my shadow. Many of my past life choices were now transparently linked to what I couldn't know. It made sense that I had chosen to work with emotionally wounded children, children who embodied what I could not know about myself.

When I began working with children, I met and worked with Gordon Richiusa. Then and now I believe Gordon and I share a commitment to facilitate the healing, learning and growth of those who seek what we can offer. Gordon has always played a unique role in my life. He seeks connection with me almost always when shadow is at my doorstep. He "appeared" during this passage of my 30th year. In the years that followed I began my long journey to understand what I had experienced and what I had discovered. In my quest I studied both traditional and nontraditional, Western, Eastern and Native American teachings. To stay in the *market place* I opted for the Western traditional path and became a licensed clinical social worker. In this role I able to fulfill my commitment as healer, seeker, artist, and privilege witness for those who invite me to participate as a lamplighter in their journey. This honorable role enriches my path - enhancing my seeking, learning, growing and healing. If my story or “message in a bottle” speaks to you I can be contacted through Five Birds Publishing.

When Gordon asked me to be a contributor to the “MESSAGE IN A BOTTLE” PROJECT, I was initially very honored and soon after impacted by the daunting prospect of succinctly capturing what I believe to be meaningful enough to offer others. Gordon’s invitation came at a time when once again, I was being prompted by life to reevaluate the truths I believe in. The solace I have at such times comes from “knowing” that an examined life reveals both what one knows and what one does not know. Baring this paradox in mind, I offer this perspective- today.

My early childhood and my subsequent life experiences taught me, that I was best served by embracing and valuing both the “good” and “bad” of my life, my sense of self and others. My life‘s path directed me to master my inner world to be able to be present in our shared world; that many of my battles, threats, dangers and seeming enemies I embraced and confronted to resolution and acceptance in my inner realm with corresponding results in our shared realm.

Much of what I believe and want to share from my journey is captured in the following sentence and ideas: ***When you stand in the light you will see your shadow*.”**

Embrace your shadow – both your light and dark have purpose and merit. As you embrace your shadow, acceptance will gift you with appreciation of self and others, giving you a means to end suffering, fear and harmful energy or actions; that through the gateway of your shadow you will see your light again and the light of others; that this appreciation dissolves judgment – the great separator; that the duality of this plane expressed in every aspect of life and individual mandates recognition and balance both within yourself and with all of life. Aspire to appreciate the lessons your circumstances have provided – find how you are served by the seeming undesired; that once you are "awake", you understand and commit to self awareness, self responsibility and what you create; that there are many paths and if yours is one of self discovery it will reveal challenge, triumph, uncertainty, change, wonderment, love and trust of self and life, and just as much humor and irony you need.

In my life Gordon has often brought me reasons to be grateful and this was another. Thank you, for giving me this opportunity.

Note: The symbol at the beginning of this essay is Ms. Arvelo's artistic representation of the themes expressed by the words. Maria Arvelo is a licensed Therapist and works as a social worker in Ventura County.

NOTE: the following abstract is also from the original, Go Tao Chi *and is written by Gordon Richiusa*

Illness & Disease Vs. Recovery and Healing

Inevitably, when people begin to discuss universal truths, the conversation often moves onto spiritual matters and from there, the topics of injury and disease will come into play. "How is it possible that The Spirit allows us to become sick or injured?" someone will ask.

I have an explanation for this, but it may not be the kind of thing that many who ask the question want to hear. For, you see I do not think that The Spirit—or whatever term you use to name the unfathomable wonders of the unknown—views the universe as human beings do. I may be wrong, but that is my impression.

Although I truly believe in the existence of a higher awareness (I cannot conceive that humanity is the pinnacle of awareness), I am hard pressed to visualize some big human sitting above it all, focused entirely on what is going on here on the planet Earth. When people say that we were created in God's image, I view that to mean that we are like shadows of the Spirit (created in its image), that we have similar properties or are essentially "like" the unknowable, and that the laws or forces that guide the Universe—or perhaps have been set in motion by The Creator—are the same ones that all sentient beings, including humans must follow. It is not the other way around. We do not get to create the Universe (or multi-verse) and the forces that guide it in our image.

Within this, I believe that the universal laws that we follow also bind the Spirit. It follows that, the Five Principles of Everything rule all awareness, just as the Spirit created the Five Principles for human beings to follow these must be patterns, or laws that it follows.

Therefore, I am forced to conclude that The Spirit has not created an atmosphere of ill health, injury or disease. By the same token, I can also conclude that when we become sick or have an accident that this is not part of any Master Plan, but rather an example of the form of humanness. In other words, we cannot blame any version of a superior being for our human misfortunes. If the Principles of Everything apply, then the Principle of Benefit must be true. The Spirit wants *us* to be healthy, well and flowing with energy of success as it would want itself to be healthy, well and flowing with energy. It is our responsibility to become aware of our own place in the grand scheme of things, not the responsibility of The Grand Ultimate to make sure that no human has nothing to be concerned about on a human level. Learning how to be happy within the context of being human (to be in the flow of humanness) is our responsibility. In other words, I think that any Higher Awareness teaches mostly by example. That is the image in which we were created. Also, without sounding overly optimistic and new-agey, adversity often appears to be the best way to learn some of the more important lessons. I have had many students fail my classes and then retake them merely because they wanted to succeed in that particular experience, rather than settle for a passing grade in a different class. Usually, on the first day of writing class, for example I tell the class that my expectations are probably higher than they were intending, but that they will benefit from the experience beyond just becoming better writers.

The Five Birds and Go-Tao-Chi symbols both are represented by what many, wrongly believe to be a yin-yang symbol. The truth is that the circle, half black and half white represents a half moon. This symbol was selected to show an ever changing, human condition. We say that each individual is like some phase of the moon. The full moon represents an intense energy. The new moon is mysterious and unfathomable. The half moon is a delicate balance, rigid with aspects of all the other phases but teeming with potential. Remember, however that the moon is never in a stagnant phase. It is always changing, either getting brighter or less luminous. We are like the moon, regardless of which stage we resemble the most, because we are always changing. In the end, the brief awareness our life force will not only bind together all the awareness of our spiritual, mental and physical beings but will be, in a sense nourished by itself and each of the individual parts or phases. Here I am led to say a few more words on Acupressure, Massage and Motionless Meditation as they are directly related to the concept of "chi" but are at a different end of the spectrum where one might consider "martial arts" to be.

There are basically two ways to meditate...active and passive. Both, in my opinion have similar (if not exact) ultimate goals. However, the debate has always existed that one form is superior to the other. A friend of mine, a teacher of Zen Meditation named John Harrison, (AKA The Blue Dragon) and I have participated in this debate for some time and he is better qualified, in my opinion to take up the banner of Zazen or seated meditation. However, I think that a word needs to be said about the different art forms that deal with the manipulation or just the experience of Chi.

In that regard, I will discuss The Five Principles from the perspectives of rehabilitation and recovery, as these are things that I have first-hand experience with and which John Harrison is also well versed (his comments appear at the end of this section). In 1982 I experienced a severe knee injury that required surgery. My doctor (at the time) told me that I would have to give up martial arts, especially kicking. These days, I love to lift my leg up in front of an audience and tell them “my doctor says I can't do this.”

In 2001 I had two accidents (a car accident and an industrial one, where a box of books tore my rotator cuff). The auto accident injured my spine and caused a concussion. The second injury was to my right shoulder. Unfortunately, these injuries prevented me from standing on one leg, lifting my arms above my head or turning my body (all necessary skills in all forms of martial arts practice). For the first time in my life, I was unable to practice the arts that I'd always relied upon to maintain health. At least, that was what I thought.

I believe that medical practices, modern surgeries and advances in medications are all examples of the modern-day miracles. We have always possessed a boundless ability to master our mind and body and I believe that the desire to be healthy and well is a strong indication that our Spiritual Guide (however that happens to manifest itself, for each individual) wants us to be healthy and happy.

From this point of view, the only thing that any medicine can accomplish is to help one return an out-of-sync flow of chi to its normal, healthy flow. All forms of direct chi manipulation (including meditation, acupuncture or massage) serve the exact same purpose as any martial art with slight differences.

When I was injured more seriously, I needed to learn to follow my own advice, and in a different way than I was used to. I had to learn to accept multiple paths to the same end. I had learned a small amount about Chua Ka, a Mongolian form of massage, which concentrates on the joints and had some experience with acupuncture and tai chi from sources such as Marshall Ho.

The pain in my spine and head required drastic measures, so I endured six epidural injections that had temporary results. I had already tried physical therapy, acupuncture and even Go-Tao-Chi with limited success. After all, I was in too much pain to relax and I needed to relax to get the full benefit of these therapies. In the end, I realized that epidurals (or other medications), acupuncture, massage and physical therapy all dealt with chi and healing from an *external* standpoint. That is, there was an outside force being applied to my body in an attempt to return the flow of chi to as natural a state as possible. With Go-Tao-Chi (or tai chi, or even yoga) the manipulation of chi is internally produced, but my body was not in a place to transcend the physical pain to allow healing to occur. I had to accept the responsibility that my choices of driving a car and being a part of the artificial, human concept of "working for a living" had put my body into circumstances that led to physical injury. It was not God that injured me, but petty, selfish, human choices.

After that, I learned to accept help of all types and from many sources to deal with new conditions that had arisen in my life. I also needed to develop a whole new perspective on success. What was once an easily achievable horizon had perhaps become an unrealistic goal. As I was getting older, my body was never going to regain the same levels of healing of which it once was capable. I needed to learn to be grateful for any progress and to realize that being grateful was actually the most powerful medicine that The Spirit had made available to me.

That is when I learned the true meanings of humility and thankfulness.

I learned the humility of a vulture, something that I had been professing for many years. You see, the vulture is a bird that flies as high as any eagle, yet makes its nest on the ground. It is also a bird that knows that to benefit fully, with its strengths and weaknesses, it must cooperate with other birds. One vulture, alone would have a hard time piercing the flesh of its prey. That is why we see vultures circling above their feasts. They are signaling other vultures to come along to assist, and partake in the meal. They need each other to pull apart the meat; since their claws are not as strong as an eagle's (for instance) it takes two birds to unveil their sustenance.

They also do not turn up their noses at any meal. No kill is too small, or too old for them to benefit from. Many birds have a preference for their meals, and there are some forms of eagle, for instance, that only eat living fish (the osprey), which often puts them into jeopardy. Hawks kill on the fly, like no other animal. The crow (the bird) was admired by one group of Native Americans, because the bird would steadfastly remain in a territory that they considered home. Whole flocks of crows sometimes could be found frozen to death in a favorite tree that they refused to leave. However, the vulture travels great distances accepting thankfully any gift that is placed upon its path.

In 1995 in created a non-profit that was organized around the Five Principles. It was called Redwood Recovery. We gave jobs to men and women in recovery from drug and alcohol addiction. The job was to plant redwood trees and to build walkways that we deemed *segments on The Path of Redwood Recovery*. Sometimes, on planting assignments, groups of workers would hold 12 step meetings. We did not discourage this activity. However, our ultimate purpose was to "start the healing and recovery processes from as positive a point as possible." When a recovered alcoholic or addict returns to the place that they planted redwood trees, they can point proudly to their loved ones and say, "This is part of my Path or Recovery."

Addiction and Awareness (a brief outline) Inspired by the Five Principles of Everything and Gestalt Awareness Practice

By John Harrison

As a counselor in the field of addiction treatment I draw from many experiences, disciplines, and methods in my work to serve my clients. Addiction is a universal scourge and is certainly reinforced in our western culture where we can get anything, anytime we want it! The overwhelming amount of information we are exposed to every day, combined with the mind-numbing speed with which we receive it, can make it easy to lose awareness of this present moment. Along with our minds, ones physical body too can become detached as we 'attach' ourselves to our computers, our 'smart' phones, our televisions and, of course, the various substances we use and abuse!

In this age where our lives seem to be accelerating, our stress also naturally seems to be increasing. In addition to addictive behaviors potentially having a strong genetic link, it's no wonder so many of us crave avoidance and escape. According to the U.S. Substance Abuse and Mental Health Services Administration, one in eight Americans suffers with addictive behaviors regarding drugs or alcohol and it costs society approximately 250 billion dollars per year.

When an individual is caught up in the cycle of addictive behavior, there is often an inability to accept whatever is being felt in the present moment and the mind is constantly wandering onto the next *fix*. In the present moment, distressing thoughts and emotions can feel like unwanted guests that we can't seem to get away from. In our *twisted and ineffective* attempt to avoid this distress, we actually amplify stress and uncomfortable emotions such as sadness, frustration, irritation, shame, or guilt. These uncomfortable emotions often kick us into a state of mind*lessness* or auto-pilot where we're unaware of our environment and more susceptible to triggers, cravings and urges.

Victor Frankl, respected psychiatrist, holocaust survivor, and author of *Man's Search for Meaning* once said: *"Between a stimulus and a response there is a space. In that space is our power to choose our response. In our response lay our growth and our freedom.*"

Is there a way to slow time down to be more aware of that space and choice? Whether our addictions have to do with alcohol, drugs, food, sex, gambling, emailing, shopping, or other injurious habit, the addictive behavior is often preceded by some triggering event that sets off a flurry of uncomfortable thoughts, feelings and sensations, leading to cravings and urges to engage in the addictive behavior. An important part of recovery is being able to recognize our triggers and how cravings and urges manifest in our bodies and minds.

As soon as we have this awareness, we have become present and stepped outside of the automatic reactive cycle that enslaves us the next moment. The present moment is that close. Many people have reported that the actual peak of an urge is about 20-30 minutes. We can learn to bring an attentive eye of curiosity and non-judgment to the feelings and thoughts as we watch them come and go.

There are many ways to bring about the state of what is called *mindfulness*. With my patients I use a very simple (but not always easy) time-tested method which springs from the wonderful synergy of Zen meditation (zazen) and Gestalt Awareness Practice....*Applied Awareness* if you will!

Simple Awareness Practice

After you learn it, you can do it anyplace or anytime that you have the chance. It can become a lifelong practice. Find someplace comfortable to sit or lie down. Take a deep breath and relax. You can keep your eyes open. Then follow these instructions: Become aware of your experience, in the sense that you exist *here and now*. Become aware that you are living this experience—doing it, observing it, or getting bored with it-—*right now*, in the present. ***Decide that you will pay attention to all of your experiences***—the internal as well the external, thoughts as well as sensations, those about the past as well as those about the future, those that are wishes or desires, those that are anxious or demanding, those that you deliberately produce, and those that seem to occur spontaneously. With regard to every experience you have, say to yourself: "Now I am aware of …"

You can start this way, by saying to yourself something like: "Now I am aware that I am sitting here. Now I am aware that I want to do this awareness experiment. Now I am aware of hesitating, asking myself what to do first. Now I am aware of a sound from outside. Now I am looking out the window" and so on. Continue in this way for a couple of minutes, watching your awareness as it unfolds. This is a *practice*…and must be...well practiced as with any skill you are trying to perfect or improve upon. It gets more familiar and effective as we go deeper into it!

I have found this practice of non-judgmental present moment awareness (a.k.a. mindfulness) an effective tool for helping patients in becoming more attuned to triggers, cravings, and urges to help break the cycle of addictive behavior. Of course, this is easier said than done. For, when struggling with an addiction it is all too common to switch onto autopilot with little or no awareness of the thoughts, feelings, and sensations that can tip one off balance and bring on that next moment of grasping.

Here are three things to bring more awareness to:

1) Body-Feeling State—It helps to be aware of emotions and how they manifest in the body. 2) Addictive Thought Styles—Common mind traps arise in connection with the body-feeling state. For example, denial, blaming, and rationalizing! 3) Negative Interpretations—When caught in an addictive cycle, we usually engage in interpreting events for the worse, which helps tip us off balance and become more susceptible to autopilot. The trick here is to just simply be aware of any of this when it arises without judging it. Start to notice how these three things are interconnected. See if you can try some of this the next time you have an craving or an urge to get on the Internet or get back to that text when,

in the moment, your relaxation or a loved one might need you more. Each time we are able to successfully use mindfulness to ride out the craving to engage in our addictive behavior–our cravings or urges become less frequent and less intense and we become stronger, more confident, and more in control of our own lives.

Mastery, Mistakes and the Process of Learning

by Ralph R Villani, Ed.d

My name is Ralph R Villani. I am Gordon Richiusa's Uncle. His Mother is my sister. Of course, I have known Gordon since his birth. I consider him a favorite relative I admire him for how he has made such a success of his life and how he has succeeded in becoming a scholar and well known educator.

Gordon asked if I would read his latest project, "the Five Principles of Everything" and react to the book. I also read his published novel, *Shidoshi The Four Ways of the Corpse*. This novel indeed is a suspense-thriller. Although Gordon explains that his goal of the Five Principles of Everything was to teach people and eventually good teachers of martial arts, I was able to relate these principles to what ever success I have had as an educator, a teacher, assistant high school principle, elementary principle, assistant superintendent, a district superintendent, a college trustee, an elected member of the Board of Directors of CalRTA, and as a member of the Los Angeles County Grand Jury.

My successful experiences in life included being elected to the Santa Monica Community College Board of Trustees from 1990 to 1994. After I retired from a school district in 1991 I joined the California Retired Teachers Association (Cal/RTA). I quickly became a leader in this organization and now serve on the State Board of Directors. Just after my retirement I was appointed by a Superior Court Judge to serve a one-year full time term on the Los Angeles County Grand Jury. I hold a Bachelor's and Master's degree from the University of Southern California and a Doctorate Degree from the University of Northern Colorado in Educational Management.

Gordon and I have discussed the definition of what is truly an educator. Gordon leans to the idea that to be an educator of students, one must deal directly with students. I contend that an outstanding administrator is one who motivates teachers in order to improve education and who knowingly or unknowingly, consistently applies the Five

Principles of Everything: Awareness, Flow, Form, Benefit and Harmony.

After I retired in 1991 I was asked by a school district in Southern California to fill in as an elementary principal while the district looked for a new principle. It was really a great experience. However, the school was not doing well. Test scores were below average. I spent almost all of my time visiting classrooms, not as an evaluator of the teacher, but to get to know what the problems might be. I determined in a few weeks that teachers were really not aware of the problems, were not working harmoniously together, did not see how working together to improve student might be a benefit to them.

During the next few weeks, I met with teachers. We had open discussions on how we might turn things around. Every suggestion was recorded. We talked about how we all would feel if test scores improved. Teachers began to work together as a team. And when the next test scores were reported, there was significant improvement. All the staff needed was someone to motivate them to do what they themselves wanted to do to help students learn. I did not know it at the time, but the Five Principles of Everything were now guiding learner growth. Teachers were meeting individual student needs, there was evidence of teachers taking on responsibility to students, teachers were making learning interesting, and they were working together as a team.

NOTE: The following comments are often given, in some form or another to new students in any classroom where Gordon Richiusa teaches, regardless of the discipline and especially for curriculum developers or teachers. What you have here is only a portion of an often given lecture. This was not part of the original Go Tao Chi. *If you use these words in your own classes, or writing, please be certain that you as you cite the source properly.*

Something to Think About

By Gordon Richiusa

I have been a professional educator for more than 25 years, teaching at the elementary, secondary and community college levels. I spent 20 years working as an educator in the L.A. County Jails, working with the inmates in high school subjects and GED preparation, as well as administering the test and coordinating the curriculum for Hacienda La Puente Adult School. My Master of Arts degree is in English Literature. I have a clear, lifetime teaching credential. Prior to that I worked in residential treatment with people of all ages, including a stint as a high school teacher in one of these facilities.

When I say that I have been a professional educator, I know that there are some who are *not* teachers and still believe that they also are educators. These people apparently surmise that if they are engaged in any aspect of the *business* of education, then they too are educators. To say it bluntly, based upon the Five Principles of Everything, this is simply not the case. For the sake of semantic agreement, only those who are on the front lines, actively engaged on a daily basis with students (for example teachers, counselors, librarians, mentors, tutors)—or ARE students themselves, pursuing knowledge or learning something in particular—can call themselves educators. In other words, only the people whose primary goal is education are really educators.

So, for the sake of our talk today, most administrators, board members, school janitors, and most clerical staff—although employed in the support-fields of educational institutions—are not educators, just as the guys who sell hot dogs at a ballpark are NOT baseball players, or hot dog executives, but should be proud to be vendors engaged in the service industry.

In addition, politicians—regardless of title or how closely they control education funding—cannot be educators unless they have a classroom and curriculum or they are students in a classroom with curriculum.

As usual, words, their denotation and their connotations, are an important concern for me. Today I'd like to differentiate between two more words: *Zen* and *Tao*. Neither one is a religion unto itself. Taoism is the belief that the

Universe runs according to definite rules and principles and that the "why" of a conduct of behavior is more important than the “who, what or when” of it.

Zen, on the other hand, generally defines a particular method for achieving a certain *end (such as enlightenment)*...even though the *end* (or goal) is at times vague and shifting. Zen is usually associated with Buddhism, but is not exclusive to it.

With that, let’s examine today’s goal. I like to boil everything down to the essential parts, using the Five Principles, as the both the starting point and the ultimate objective. These “essence statements” go by many names. I call them: Concept Training or Capsule Reviews. The capsule of any endeavor is the essential parts of the defining characteristics that summarize what the related principle is and how it relates to what we are trying to accomplish.

For instance, the essential concepts of business are probably 1) Supply and Demand and 2) Profit vs. loss. The essential parts of writing, speaking or reading are: 1) Communication and 2) Audience. The essential knowledge for swimming are:1) Buoyancy and Newtonian physics. The essential parts of governing are: 1) security and 2) cooperation.

It is possible to turn any of these into a meditation but to do so, we must be certain that all five principles are being considered, and more importantly that none are being violated. In this way we elevate what we are doing (hopefully engaging one on the levels Mind, Body and Spirit) to a whole new plane. In other words, our thinking about our discipline, our actions related to it and the perspective from which we view this relationship—in the way that being a teacher or being a student, might allow you to become a TRUE educator—can alter the most mundane into the sublime. Anything can become a meditation.

In my classrooms, I give this information to students on the first day so that they can begin to understand where I am coming from.

A Positive Attitude

by Renee Baribeau/ The Practical Shaman

Hello, my name is Renee Baribeau; today is January 10, 2012. I am known as The Practical Shaman, and my role as shaman is that of weaving our global village—of bringing peace to our world by healing one person at a time. I have been asked here to offer an insightful message to someone who will find it five decades from now. What do I feel is most important that they know?

First and foremost, we must all live our lives trusting in the future, planning to sustain the earth's resources for our children and all other living beings. No matter when this message is found, children will forever remain our legacy.

As a baby boomer, I grew up in a generation in which parental roles dramatically shifted with a monumental consumer revolution. Women left their children at home to enter the work force, and the traditional understanding of a nuclear family unit was forever shaken to its core. My childhood was cut short as responsibilities to care for my younger sibling became a necessity. Not only was I unable to play freely like my predecessors, but while unattended, I was also a victim of abuse. Subsequently, my life passion has included healing these wounds for myself and countless other victims. It is important we remember that children will forever need time to play in a nourishing, safe environment with loving adult role models.

Make no mistake, no matter what changes come to pass on this earth, optimistic awareness bears a difference. Our commitment and responsibility to all beings who will take over this planet that we will bequeath to them is key. In my generation's childhood, little was considered gainful in raising young ones to be conscious caretakers of their world. The attention pendulum has swung to the other extreme, and once again parents are consciously focused on their progeny. Presently, in 2012, individuals are waking up and exploring their lost connection to the planet and other people. Our children are more awake. We must return the lost art of playing, music, and creative expression to our schools to perpetuate this awakening.

I've also come to realize it is necessary to look and see what we are doing right. We are so quick to point the finger at what we need to do differently; I genuinely believe that identifying what we are doing right is equally as important. Yes, we've devastated this earth. But at this very moment, we are focused on helping our children thrive. We're actively working at creating community, building gardens, and heading full circle back to a time before the industrial revolution—a time when we understood the importance of our earth and cultivating the land.

There is a monumental movement right here, in my lifetime, to go back to the simple things. For years, I chased after my own popularity and my own idea of the person I would be when saying something important. Now I realize that's not the measure of who I am; the measure of who I am is how I live in balance with the earth, within myself, and within my community. What I've personally come back around to experience is that I live today present. I live today in simple joy. It is difficult to fathom all that I had to trip around to get back to the simple concept that how I do anything is how I do everything. So, for today, I may just get up and go out to weed my garden—and that's exactly enough.

For a very, very long time, I realized the need to gather a group of holistic practitioners in order to truly know our doctors and lawyers are the heart-centered people with whom we actually want to do business. As a result, six years ago I began building a holistic network, one that continues to grow today. And in doing so, I realized we were preaching to the choir. I realized that at this time and space we've all come to this gate together, and that no matter who you are or what you are doing, you are participating in the awakening. After two thousand years of living in the dark, we are waking up to who we really are. What I find particularly funny is that who we really are now is not so different from who we really were two thousand years ago, when the things that mattered were our families, our communities, and our service to the earth.

So, if you are finding this message two hundred years from now, or even two thousand years from now, and you have some way of translating this message into your life, I really just want to pose one Question: What are you doing right?

Natural Human Interaction and Core Human Values

By Gordon Richiusa

There is a group of Buddhist monks who live at the base of Mt. Fuji, Japan who feel (as I do) that the natural act of running is the easiest way to achieve a meditative state for those who are able bodied. Everyday, the devotees at the monastery run or walk approximately the distance of a marathon. In the morning they run to the mountain's peak. Then, in the evening they run down the hill to their temple.

I have routinely used running, walking, hiking, and climbing as methods for transforming the attention of a student from themselves onto the five principles.

In the early 1980's I was learning from a group known as Four Directions, run by a Lakota Sioux pipe-carrier, Ernie Longwalker. Through that group I participated in the sacred sweat lodge or inipi ceremony and was allowed to attend a sharing of ceremonies on the Navaho reservation in Arizona, where I witnessed (among other things) a Sundance conducted by the famous Leonard Crow Dog.

Prior to the Sundance, there was an Indian 10K run for which many of the young bucks were conditioning themselves to participate. This particular event had the added attraction of participation from the Taramara tribes of southern Mexico. This tribe of natives is well known for their ability to run long distances and had sent some young men and one or two of its elders to show support for the event. We were sitting around, the night prior to the 10K when I decided to try and make conversation with one elder who looked to be in his late 70s or 80s. "Can you still run long distances?" I asked.

Through an interpreter, the old man gave this answer, "I'm very old now and I don't run like I used to. Now, I could run today, tomorrow and part of the next day...but that's all."

Besides being very funny in a typically Aboriginal sort of way, this comment served to show me how different cultures can view the same activities from very different perspectives.

To the old Taramaru, running was simply a way of life. When you get old, whatever the activity you will slow down, but you only stop doing whatever it is that keeps you alive, when you are dead. Running, or any other activity that you feel is healthful, should be viewed as beneficial (not exercise) all of our lives changing only as conditions require. Within any category or discipline, hierarchies and further regimentation of expertise will develop. For instance, I used to like to run on ridges. I felt that this was the finest form of running. Ridge Running allowed me maximum access to an awareness of the Five Principles because it forced me into a heightened awareness. On the ridge, a trail that was literally on top of a range of mountains or hills, allowed me to focus my attention on the trail in from of me, the horizon above the trail and on the perceptual anomaly on both sides of the road, due to the drop off on both sides. As with Archery, I could "get into that almost hypnotic state" very quickly because I was forced to pay close attention to details while, at the same time expand my awareness to see the bigger picture.

Running on trails, tracks, cross-country running, hiking, walking, trekking are all "levels" of the natural ability (and desire) that all humans seem to have. Everything else is just another example of our tendency to turn everything into a source of socialization or conflict.

Rather than dwell on this point, let's say that the "best" systems, running or otherwise, seem to be those that require no extra equipment or circumstance beyond what is natural or easily accessible (keeping in mind variations in abilities and physical or mental, or emotional limitations).

I have worn a great many hats in my lifetime, as teacher, academic researcher, writer and motivator. All hats have a relationship to the other hats. All my activities have been modified by circumstances in life. I no longer ridge run, but I still travel from point A to point B (usually on a very flat surface, and not very fast, though I still call it running) with the same level of intensity. Now I might trot along a beach at low tide one day and the next run the same basic trail at high tide. Both of these experiences, though similar are very different, emphasize the use of different muscles and offer varied benefits. This willingness to modify every lesson and experience, to see it from all angles and to appreciate the lessons learned has been my salvation.

During the time that I was teaching martial arts with intensity, I created a non-profit organization called, Redwood Recovery. This group gave jobs to people in recovery, primarily drugs and alcohol. The jobs were all focused on planting redwood trees (sequoia) throughout California. These were paying jobs, which was something different than what others may have been trying to accomplish. Everywhere that we planted sequoia trees, of any number of genus, we put in a walking path, and plaques that designated the area as part of our Path of Recovery.

Many of my black belt, or other level tests were conducted in wilderness areas so that we could test a student's endurance and his other related skills at the same time. Naturally, I eventually networked my interests and started advertising when and where or the other of the events would take place. I called the event, THIS IS NOT A RACE. The grand scale metaphor was this: Life is not a race. We all meet along the same pathways. Some are walking these paths to heal old wounds, and others for other reasons. We would give certificates to those who "showed up" at the starting line. You did not have to go anywhere else than the starting line to get a certificate. There was no set course, other than the ones that each individual group, for various reasons wanted to establish.

My injury forced me to see everything from a different perspective. When I first learned of Tai Chi and a form of massage called Chua Ka, I did not realize how important perspective was in Applying Awareness. I need to take a moment to thank all of the talented massage therapists and acupuncturists who helped me to overcome injury and chronic pain with the gift of their touch.

When you first saw the title of this section, you probably did not think that I would be talking about massage. However, now that I am, it may be that our interest is piqued. Many people either love to get a massage or feel that they have a special gift to give them. Either way, the fact that from both ends of the spectrum the idea that massage could be considered a form of meditation might be appealing to you. The reason for this is that massage, like running, or tai chi, or yoga, or seated meditation or prayer, or just sitting and thinking are all activities that stem from our natural human tendencies.

Tai Chi is a Chinese form of martial arts, which emphasizes a meditative state, accomplished through performing certain movements, often in a particular order. As with yoga postures, you need no special equipment or even a partner to practice the form.

Note: It is generally considered inappropriate to acknowledge oneself as a "master" of tai chi, since this is a very personal form of exercise and there is no rank status associated with this practice.

In addition, I would like to point out that this book does not support or oppose any particular religious movement. However, if you have read the book Go-Tao-Chi, the five principles of chi, then you know that while I am opposed to religious practice, in general, I fully support ANY religion, meditative practice or art form which assists an individual in a greater understanding of their positive place in the world. Also, the principles and techniques expressed here can be applied to any spiritual and/or religious belief system. In other words, I make a distinction between "spiritual" and "religious" concepts. I am not a Buddhist, Christian, Atheist, Zionist, Muslim, or Warlock (etc.). I do, however believe strongly that an awareness of our spiritual selves, however that is accomplished, is essential for true happiness. If that means that a person fully embraces a religious perspective, then I say GREAT!

Let us simply agree here, that massage can be the vehicle by which a heightened state of awareness may be achieved that is natural and also utilizes our desires for human contact as part of the benefit. For me, a fully heightened state of awareness is more easily achieved only when one is both completely focused and fully open at the same time.

Specific techniques for achieving this state are taught in many martial arts classes. To quickly advance beyond an argument on this subject, I have introduced a training technique to my classes. I fill up to five similar looking bean bags with varied weights and sizes of objects. For instance, in one I have about three pounds of steel shot mixed in with actual beans. In another I have some sort of packing material (cloth or faux fur these days) or large (up to one inch in diameter) wooden balls. In each case the "sound" and the "look" of the bean bags is as close to identical as possible. The object of the "game" is to throw and catch the bags, with both hands. You play with at least one partner (I've had as many as twenty people and twenty bags in a group) so bags are flying in and out of your hands rapidly. You must learn to throw accurately with each hand, and catch with both hands as well. Here's the catch: You must throw and catch each bag differently. After convincing a person that this is possible—because they learn to function well within the parameters of this juggling act that perhaps only a few second earlier they were not convinced was physically possible—I always ask the question: Since you are catching each bag differently, when do you make the determination about HOW you are going to accomplish this task and still keep the throws accurate?' This question forces the participant to understand the concept of "expanding and focusing our awareness at the same time."

When a heightened state is achieved during a massage, the patient often expresses that something indefinable has taken place. I have heard it said of certain therapists, "I just love him/or her. I wish I could take them home with me. I've never felt so good."

As a massage or physical therapist, you know that there are times when you "really feel like you've connected" with a client. I believe that to be a good massage therapist is a calling that springs from the most simple of human understanding. When something hurts, we rub it. When we rub it, the pain gets better. Both the person who does the rubbing and the person who gets rubbed feel a connection with the fundamental source of goodness and power that is at the core of the Universe. In other words, if done in the proper spirit, massage, therapy or any healthful interaction can indeed be a form of meditation just as any "dance" or movement can be enhanced by coordinated effort.

Body Systems/The Trinity of Chi

All forms of medicine, both Eastern and Western, deal with the body as a unity of various systems. We have the skeletal, muscular, vascular, nervous and digestive systems for instance. The difference (if we want to call it that) is that the Eastern way of looking at things assumes one overlaying system, which both reflects and reacts to all the other systems. This is the system of Chi, or energy/spirit from which all other systems flow. Eastern medicine is reliant upon eastern philosophy in this regard but this "multiple layers of reality" are often accepted as fact by even the most complicated scientific and spiritual beliefs.

Today, we hear of the unity of Mind, Body and Spirit as if these three aspects of ourselves are somehow separate or that the concept is new or the exclusive domain of one particular belief system. The truth is if you remove any one line on this triangle, then the triangle no longer exists. Many cultures and beliefs are founded on the understanding of this trinity (everything from Zen Buddhism to Christianity).

In education, it is well known that people learn (and teach) best through one or more "modalities." These include Visual, Auditory and Tactual. In other words, some people like to have things shown to them, others like to hear explanations, while others favor diving in with both hands.

In massage, we know that the addition of soft music and certain fragrances will enhance the experience for some people. Indeed, any professional massage therapist has experienced clients who may actually tense at the touch of a hand. The music or a soothing word from the therapist is required to break through the barrier of resistance that people may have built around themselves. Teachers learn to teach the same lesson in a variety of ways, while massage therapists must respond to the needs of the clients through the same modalities.

At the same time, there are numerous methods, techniques and schools of thought for the best way to make contact with the client. Usually, there is at least a basic acceptance of the various levels of awareness on which our actions affect one another. I have heard it said, for instance that a therapist must “feel love” for the patient. There are some accepted forms of meditation, which indeed require interaction between two people (the Kata Sutra is one famous example).

In another section of this book we will learn the basics of Chua Ka, which is a Mongolian warrior's form of massage that concentrates on the skeletal system and which was usually done in pairs or groups prior to a battle.

There are other massage techniques that deal mainly with the muscles, or the glands or the chakras or pressure points or meridians. Regardless of the point of orientation, or the techniques being used, Massage can be a meditative experience for either or both the patient and the person giving the massage. And, to achieve optimum results, mind, body and spirit must be in perfect harmony.

Manipulating Chi

Based upon an agreement on the basic concepts expressed in the first two chapters, we come to the point in this text where we define what it is that all forms of the healing arts have in common. Whether it is Tai Chi, Yoga, acupuncture, acupressure, chiropractic or massage therapy, Western or Eastern medicine each "art" or "science" generally attempts to manipulate one or more of the systems and therefore, according to our definitions, attempts to manipulate chi. The differences are in orientation and point of departure.

Again we are forced to use common terms to make our points. In this case the basic perspectives are known as "internal" or "soft" and its opposite "external" or "hard." In all cases, whether a practitioner is shooting arrows, using a sword, throwing punches, kicks, balls or boomerangs, running a business, catching a wave or just watching one, sitting in different poses under a banyan tree, writing a paragraph, essay or poem, solving an equation or giving (or getting) a massage, they are merely finding ways to become aware of Universal Energy (spirit), using a coordination of their Technique (Mind) and their physical being (Body).

Remember, too that these terms (like all the others in this book) are just ways for us to discuss the concepts. The only true value of any concept is in the experience of it. Therefore, the only way to benefit from what is written here is to experience it for you.

For our purposes, let's say that Yoga and Tai Chi are examples of an “internal” manipulation of chi, while massage, chiropractic and acupuncture are examples of an “external” manipulation.

This simply means that no outside external force (another person, chemical or device such as needles) is needed to achieve a heightened awareness.

Massage, on the other hand appears to be for those who are tactually oriented. In other words, to truly “get the full message” a tactual person has to physically “touch” the lesson.

For the tactual person we have developed many well-known forms of meditation, such as archery, karate and kung fu, yoga, tai chi and other spiritual or religious groups have created rituals, which allow the practitioner to “act” on their beliefs.

In Hinduism and yoga, the three “ways to worship” are known as midra, mudra and mandela. These correspond to the three ways in which we learn. Midra is anything that involves sound, including chanting, singing, bell ringing, and speaking. Mudra, is anything, which involves the body, generally the hands themselves. So, when you see pictures of the Buddha with his fingers lightly touching or movies where ninja are intertwining their hands to make themselves invisible (kuji kiri) then they are involved with mudra. Mandala is coordination with Universal Law, depicted through pictures or figures. In this category is everything from the Sistine chapel to sand painting of the Navahos.

As you can see, all spiritual and religious perspectives have sought ways to increase their awareness of and harmony with the Universal Laws. In all cases, we have chosen ways that best meet our own needs in terms of how we learn and understand.

Unfortunately, instead of acknowledging our differences in pursuit of the same ideals we have become narrow-minded basing our "ways of knowing" on a specific ritual, act or technique.

In martial arts, as an example we have people professing that their "style" is better than any other. In ancient Japan there were different schools of swordsmanship. One school recommended a medium sword, another would recommend a really long one and still another suggested that two swords be used. Of the later, the niton-ichi ryu or "two swords as one" school, the creator Myamoto Musashi had one of his most famous duels using a wet boat oar and finishing the job with his hands and feet. His recommendation, which lives as one of his basic principles of life was, "Know when to let go of the sword."

Finally, following the advice of Musashi we do not advocate Swedish massage over Reiki over any other (including the style that we will discuss next). What we do advocate is being open to discovering new and better ways to use your "art" and your "skill" (in whatever form) to become the best you can be.

I usually say here that I believe that the Universe is part of a grand-scale triangle that could be described as The Known, The Unknown and the Unknowable.

Our physical world, it is scientifically likely, is governed by the same principles as the Unknowable, but that is about all we will ever be able to know about it from our puny, little planet.

Rather than make ourselves crazy dwelling on what we cannot ever perceive, we can marvel at and perfect the interaction with the many miracles that can be experienced every day.

For the sake of this chapter we can speculate that any form of massage, which strives to balance the flow of chi (at any level) is in harmony with the basic principles of a meditative practice.

Diverse Actions—Same Focus—Chua Ka and Lomi Lomi

I have always referred to Chua Ka as the "shotgun" of acupressure because the basic concepts of each are essentially the same. Chua Ka concentrates on certain points on the body to relieve and prevent pain, while acupressure does the same. In acupressure (and on a more precise basic acupuncture) knowledge of how chi follows certain meridians throughout the body (and how one remote point can affect another) is the result of centuries of research and investigation. All systems are taken into consideration, as they relate to the flow of chi.

Chua Ka, though extremely effective, is single-minded in its approach. It was performed by Mongolian warriors prior to battle so that they would not be able to feel pain, should they be wounded during battle. It can also help to elevate pain, once injury has occurred.

For the warriors it was important to be able to "fight through the pain" so Chua ka also allows a person continued use of the muscles, while at the same time numbing them. This seemingly supernatural ability of the Mongolian warrior to ignore an injury and continue fighting was one of the main reasons that the Great Wall of China was built.

The “system” that is concentrated on in Chua Ka, is the skeleton and the major joints. This includes the spine itself and several points on the skull.

Anyone who has any body awareness or an understanding of chi, meridians and body systems knows that everything is interrelated. The ribs, for instance are covered with muscles and skin, yet house the internal organs and an intricate network of nerves and glands and other bones.

When concentrating a Chua Ka massage on the bones of the arms, the wrists, elbows and shoulders the muscles and especially the nervous system itself (at the major joints) are also massaged. Some practitioners that I've spoken to actually believe that this contact with the nervous system is what gives Chua Ka its strength. I agree that this is a likely scenario. Bones (even the thicker ones) are really somewhat spongy in nature. They only turn “hard” when they are removed from a living body. In other words, when a bone is *alive* it *gives*. The more alive it is, the more flexible and strong. How many seniors have heard from their doctors that their bones have become brittle with age?

So, when a sweeping motion is made along the arm, for instance, even when the massage is not at the elbow or wrist, the nervous system is being gently stroked. In fact, I would have to say that rubbing the nervous system "through the bones" is probably the best (and only really safe way) to make contact with it. Anyone who has ever had a disk slip or a nerve "pinched" knows that a bruised nerve can cause severe and long lasting pain.

On the other side of the coin, from the perspective of Chua Ka, the skeleton, tendons and ligaments all serve to shield the nervous system allowing for a much-muted stimulation. The effect is that a person generally feels "numb" or "tingly" with minor Chua Ka, and numb throughout the body with a lengthy treatment. The "technique" is a sweeping or hard brushing motion with the hands, which contacts the joints, muscles, pressure points then sweeps along the bones to "connect the dots." Hence, the image of the "shot gun" effect that I spoke about.

Mongolian Warriors would massage one another for hours and even several days before a battle. You can imagine that they would feel no pain for an extended period after such a massage. Just the experience of touch itself has a tendency to release a whole array of chemical reactions (both in the brain and in the muscles themselves, in the form of endomorphine) that give an individual the feeling of euphoria. Again, this includes both the person being touched and the person doing the touching.

Truly anyone can learn Chua Ka, and it is especially easy for a trained massage therapist to learn the basics and incorporate it in their own treatment programs. Naturally, one size does not fit all. Chua Ka is a great addition to the vast body of physical treatment knowledge, but I don't think it should be considered a replacement for any other form of massage.

The beauty of Chua Ka is that very little instruction is needed to perfect the skill, because it is based upon our natural inclination to "touch to heal." As long as a person has the sensitivity to follow the bones with their fingers and knows his or her own body well enough to figure out where the joints and the "sensitive spots" are, then they can do Chua Ka. In fact, Chua Ka (like acupressure) can, for the most part be performed on oneself. The only limitations would be the "hard to reach" areas, such as the middle of the back.

Lomi Lomi is the Hawaiian form of massage that I also like to teach as an example of the "soft" end of the spectrum. Here, the masseuse begins with the concept that they are "part of the process" rather than merely vehicle for pleasure of another. Lomi Lomi technique tries to imitate the natural movements that are apparent in the life of an island dweller. The hands move independently of one another and the forearms, voice (chanting or singing) and intention of both participants are integrated with the movements. A proper lomi lomi massage is a perfect example of the integration of the five principles between two (or more) people.

Naturally, I cannot teach you Chua Ka or Lomi Lomi in a short book or article such as this and will not attempt to do so. Find a teacher with knowledge of either art and apply yourself, either as a student or as a participant. In both cases, your gain will be equal to your investment. This is true of any subject or discipline.

END NOTES The Principles in Common

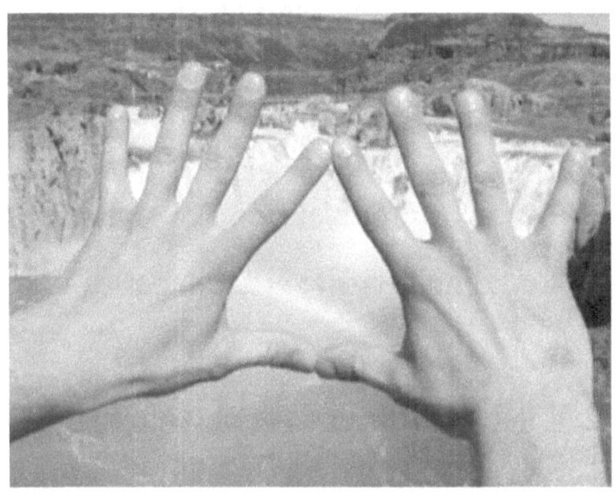

Zen Proverb: "The Universe Breathes Both Hard and Soft."

This quote begins this book and will end it (in a sense).

I have been a practitioner and student of martial arts for the past fifty years. That does NOT, by any means, make me a MASTER (since I don't believe such a state exists). However, I do believe that my experience and dedication to the study of all forms of martial arts, methods of communication, education and the psychology of being human have allowed me a unique advantage from which to make certain observations about the similarities and differences in the styles I've studied.

My method of teaching I call Concept Training, since I believe that concepts are much more important in a well rounded training program, then any particular technique, art or piece of equipment. Here are some of the concepts that I work with: 1) The discipline learned in martial arts training offers a great advantage to the success of Total Fitness. 2) the Brain is the best weapon. 3) Faith and trust in our feelings are our best prevention of having to defend ourselves. 4) Avoiding conflict is far superior to any defense technique.

I use the Okinawan form of karate known as Goju Ryu as the foundation for the empty hand training, which is the heart of the overall teaching. I have chosen this "style" as a foundation because I know it best, and because the name means "Hard-Soft Way." However, I supplement what I teach, with any form of healthful movement that a student should like to participate in. This is the foundation of Ninjitsu (a martial science that I taught for Frank Dux).

I believe in the adage: the Best form of exercise is the one that an individual will do on a regular basis. I've created my own style, The Five Bird System, based upon these beliefs.

I say that Go-Tao-Chi or The FIVE PRINCIPLE METHODOLOGY is Concept Based, because it distills various forms, ideas or disciplines (regardless of culture-of-origin) with the goal of simplifying one's own personal life strategy or exercise regimen by focusing Awareness on the relationship between Movements and the Stationary Postures. As with acupuncture, acupressure or a host of rituals or spiritual behaviors, these actions are performed in a specific way to achieve specific and nonspecific benefits (we don't know HOW it works, we just know that we feel better). In fact, as acupuncture or massage is an EXTERNAL application of these principles on the body's structure. Go-Tao-Chi strives to be an INTERNAL application of them.

We could say, in the language of martial arts that Go-Tao-Chi concentrates mainly on the relationship between Mind, Body and Spirit, or Awareness, Action and the Unknown. In many formal lines of thought a "trinity" of these three ultimate perspectives is at the core of the philosophy. In these same realms, the number 5 is also highly significant.

"In the end, the difference between Soft And Hard is the difference between being in the right place at the right time and choosing to act in proper manner, once you get there."—GFR

I did not truly understand the significance of my own words until a student of mine (grown into an adult, from the time I had the following experience with him) pointed out how this phrase had related to a joint experience we'd had. I had taken about half a dozen children "on an adventure" instead of staying in the classroom. Since none of my students had every seen Chinatown, we decided to go there. When we arrived, we saw smoke billowing out of a doorway down a cobblestone walk. "Where are we going now?" One of the children asked me, just as I spotted the smoke. "We're going down there," I said, pointing to what was becoming a special area of interest to the local inhabitants. We walked through an open door, past several people who were muttering in Chinese to one another. We entered, me at the front, kids trailing behind like a mother duck and her ducklings and saw a large wok (a giant cooking pan) in the center of a room with flames licking the low ceiling. Many men and women stood around, obviously agitated and concerned as one man came from a back room with a glass of water and threw it on the pan. This, as many of us know is not a good idea in a cooking fire and the flames seemed to be fueled even further. As the water bearer headed into the back room again I called out, "Does anyone know how to speak English?"

One man stepped through the group and answered quickly, "I speak English." To that I responded, "Ask him if he has a fire extinguisher." I pointed to the guy who was coming back with another cup of water.

The man who had stepped forward spoke in Chinese to the man with the cup of water. He ran to the back room again and returned shortly with a fire extinguisher that he handed to me. I quickly handed it to the man who spoke English. He looked at the English writing on the side, in a confused manner. I adjusted the extinguisher so that the nozzle was facing the flames as they continued to rage in the pan. "Now, pull the pin and then pull the trigger!" I said as I pantomimed what I wanted him to do. He followed my advice and quickly doused the flames.

A large crowd had gathered at the door and they all watched as the children and I walked out the door and returned to the car. "Remember this day," I told them. "This is the day that you saved Chinatown from burning to the ground."

It was years later that one of those children pointed out that "We were in the right place at the right time and we knew what to do once we got there."

In the realms of martial arts training, or massage, or life skills, or business or applying knowledge in any capacity the Five Principle Approach, should NOT be considered a discipline unto itself. It should be thought of as a kind of

Blue Print for general behavior rather than the finished house. We could also say that a Human Being is like a sailboat on a large body of water, moving with the wind.

The boat is not the wind, nor is it the water. However, to achieve its ultimate benefit, the boat must use the wind and the water to its best advantage. The boat, in a sense, must be totally self-aware. The wind and the water have many similarities, and when the boat interacts with either, we might say that it is like the wind or a slave to the water. But, neither one of these statements is ultimately true.

The more that the sailor in the boat knows about the wind or the water, or even the boat itself, will aid him or her in guiding the boat to the ultimate destination where ever that happens to be. Sometimes the water is smooth, or rough, or has strong currents, and the weight inside the boat must be shifted or the tiller (steering mechanism) must be turned slightly to compensate. The sailor and the boat, benefit from knowledge, observation of the water and intuition. If the water is warm or shallow, the boat will sail a certain way. If the water freezes or is deep, other conditions exist that must be dealt with.

With the wind, the unseen, it is the same. The focus and control of the boat to its destination can only hope for a favorable wind, then trim the sail properly to the wind that is made available. Focusing on all Five Principles of Everything makes available power, the relationship and result of the interaction of boat, wind and water, without dwelling on any one of them.

Feel free to contact me through my blog, www.5birdsmartialarts.blogspot.com or through my FREE online e-book on communication skills, http://www.vision-revision.pbwiki.com where some of my other writings are made available. I am grateful for the opportunity to share YOUR views of the contents of this book. The words here are NOT set in stone and I expect they will continue to be modified long after I am gone. However, the concept of "being grateful" appears to be one of the admirable attributes that come from following a five principled approach to life. As I have often said, I would be nothing if it were not for my teachers, and I made a promise to one many years ago that I would not diminish the importance of this concept. So, I will end this book with some words in the spirit of that teacher.

The prayer of thanks is one that we learned specifically from the Native American. The one truly Native American holiday that we all celebrate is Thanksgiving. So I will end this new edition of The Five Principles of Everything in the manner that I learned from some of my teachers.

Thank you, Grandfather Spirit.

My prayers of thanks go out in the four directions, to the four families of man...to all the generations...To the creepers and crawlers, to the plants and trees, to the four legged, the winged ones, the swimmers, the seen and unseen and to all creation, including the Earth, our mother.

I thank you for all the lessons and gifts, obstacle and adversities that have been placed upon my path of life.

I thank you for my family, friends, acquaintances, our leaders and followers, even my enemies, all those who have been my teachers or have joined with me along my way.

I thank you for allowing me to walk this path of a human being, which I will walk to the very end, wherever it leads. I will crawl, walk or run, with my head held high and my heart glad for an awareness of the five birds, the five principles and the myriad gifts that have been granted to me as a human being.

All my relations. Os. Om. Amen. Aloha.

Final Statement

By Grandmaster Alfred Urquidez

I was asked to direct the Spanish Translation of this text, which is an honor for me, although I am not Spanish or Mexican as many people believe. My family is Apache and Blackfoot. My Native name is Badger. I am the Executive Council to the Ambassadors for the Martial Arts Masters Hall of Fame and a member of a total of eight Halls of Fame myself. However, I am known more for my actions than my words. Therefore, I will keep this brief.

What I would to add from my heart is this: I, Alfred Urquidez have known Shihan Gordon Richiusa for several years now and it feels like over a century. We both have the same mind in teaching, and the same respect for martial arts concepts as guiding principles for the world. My path is to be a mentor and to teach others to be positive in any situation that comes their way. I teach to be a scholar before becoming a warrior. That is how all my other family members teach their students. How you think determines what you create in life. That is Applied Awareness. I have a love and passion for my art, Kenpo-Shotokan, a soft and hard art combined from two different styles. That is Harmony of Motion and Action. My family is the only one in the world to be certified to teach that art. This style was born in 1965, birthed by my older brother, Grandmaster Arnold Urquidez and brought to prominence by my more famous brother, Benny "The Jet" Urquidez. Together they had to get permission from both of the other arts to create the style. That is our Form. I teach the Old School Way, where mutual respect between student and teacher is needed for success. My students become part of my family. We know what *Osh* means. It's the Way of Life. As to my brother who I love and respect so much, Shihan Gordon Richiusa, I say "Osh, my brother!"

That is Benefit.

www.ingramcontent.com/pod-product-compliance
Lightning Source LLC
Chambersburg PA
CBHW061549100726
47898CB00002B/297

* 9 7 8 0 9 8 5 3 2 7 6 0 6 *